# MARINE
# COPPERSMITHING

BY
FRANK J. CARR

FIRST EDITION

McGRAW-HILL BOOK COMPANY, INC.
NEW YORK AND LONDON
1944

# Marine Coppersmithing
by Frank J. Carr

Originally published in 1944
by McGraw-Hill Book Company

Reprinted by
Lindsay Publications Inc
Bradley IL 60915

ISBN 1-55918-028-5          2011

1        2        3.        4

# WARNING

*To my wife*

WITH SINCERE APPRECIATION

OF HER HELP

# CONTENTS

# PREFACE

IT HAS often been said that coppersmithing is one trade that cannot be learned from a book; it has to be seen! That is true, and this book has been written, not to take the place of visual instruction, but to supplement it.

Coppersmithing is a complicated manual skill involving such a wide range of operations that no man can claim to know all there is to know about every part of it. There are many phases of coppersmithing, and many ways of doing each job, and the author has made no attempt to show all of them. What he has tried to do is to show what seemed to him the best and simplest way of doing marine coppersmithing.

No doubt because of its general complexity and the lack of written information about the trade, coppersmithing has been a neglected phase in the education of engineers and designers. It is hoped that this book will bring to their attention the many possibilities for efficient, streamlined design, light weight, and the saving of materials to be found in the use of copper for lines and fittings. It is also hoped that it will be of service to the men of this craft, helping them to improve the quality of their work so that they can build better ships. It is hoped, too, that this book will prove of value to the craft itself, not only during the present emergency, but afterward, by adding many skilled and competent coppersmiths to its number.

The author wishes to thank his fellow workmen at Puget Sound Navy Yard for the many ideas and suggestions that they offered from time to time.

FRANK J. CARR.

BREMERTON, WASHINGTON,
*December,* 1943.

# MARINE COPPERSMITHING

## CHAPTER I

### TOOLS AND EQUIPMENT

There has never been a successful attempt at standardizing the patterns of coppersmithing hammers because the coppersmith usually makes his own special hammers to suit the work on hand or to suit his fancy. Since one coppershop may have an entirely different type of work from another, hammers will vary in size and shape from shop to shop. Figure 1 shows the basic types of hammer used by coppersmiths. The coppersmith makes his own tools from material on hand, and so he is free to exercise his imagination and ingenuity according to his needs.

The radius of the facings is the important feature on most hammers, and for this reason the coppersmith has a dozen or so hammers from which to choose. These facings are made to fit the various types of job that the coppersmith is called upon to do. If the hammer has nicks or imperfections on the facing, the metal being hammered will take on these marks; therefore hammers must be kept smooth and free from rust and dirt. Coppersmithing hammers should not be used for hammering steel or hand tools because the polished facings may be injured. Special hammers are used for this purpose.

The basic hammer types are as follows:

**Ball-peen Hammer.**—The ball-peen hammer, sometimes called a "machinist's hammer," is the favorite all-service hammer. One end of the ball peen is rounded; the other is flat. It is used in connection with other tools such as a chisel and center punch, for hammering on steel and for various other jobs. This hammer does not have a smooth-polished facing because it is intended for ordinary rough usage.

**Bumping Hammer** (see Fig. 1).—The bumping hammer has two well-rounded ends, one slightly more rounded than the

1

other.  The coppersmith uses several sizes of bumping hammers, all with different facings and lengths.  The bumping hammer should not be used with chisels or with other tools because it must retain a smooth face.

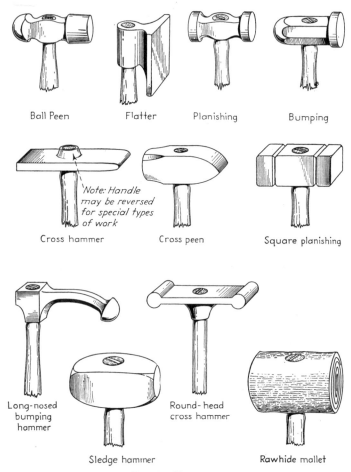

Ball Peen       Flatter       Planishing       Bumping

Note: Handle may be reversed for special types of work

Cross hammer       Cross peen       Square planishing

Long-nosed bumping hammer

Round-head cross hammer

Sledge hammer       Rawhide mallet

Fig. 1.—Hammers.

**Cross-peen Hammer** (see Fig. 1).—One end of this hammer is flat; the other end is tapered to a blunt edge at right angles to the handle.  The cross-peen hammer, like the bumping hammer, is used primarily on tools and for blacksmithing.  However, for coppersmithing uses the cross end is used for thin edging copper sheets in preparation for brazing and for working with heavy hand tools. It may also be used for all general service.

**Planishing, or Polishing, Hammer** (see Fig. 1).—The planishing hammer is used for most copper finishing work. The faces are kept highly polished. In the finish hammering, or "planishing," of copper, both the copper and the hammer face should be perfectly clean, or the dirt will be hammered into the copper. Dirt clinging to the face of the hammer also will have an undesirable result in the appearance of the finished job.

Planishing hammers are made both round and square faced to suit the nature of the work, and they come in different weights and with different facings. The coppersmith needs planishing hammers with several facings to fit various jobs.

**Cross Hammers** (see Fig. 1).—Cross hammers are as important to the coppersmith as bumping and planishing hammers. The uses vary from thin edging, planishing, and rolling in wire edges, to working out wrinkles while making balls or reducing pipe. They are also used for work on the edge of a sharp shoulder; the handles may be put in reverse, the shoulder being away from the handle, as is shown in Fig. 1.

**Flatters** (see Fig. 1).—The flatter is used in hammering rosin-filled pipe bends, in rounding pipe over a mandrel, and in performing the many operations that require a large flat-surfaced hammer. The sledge flatter is made with a convex, or an opposite concave, facing to be used with a sledge hammer, the sledge striking the flatter while the flatter is held on the pipe at the desired location.

**Long-nosed Bumping Hammer** (see Fig. 1).—Some uses of this hammer are peening brazing flanges and working small saddle branches. Any job that requires an elongated hammer, such as bumping inside a tube or cylinder, may be performed with this hammer.

**Mallets** (see Fig. 2).—The use of mallets is very important in the working of sheet copper and ordinarily is required for work on hot copper. The rawhide mallet is used for working cold copper. The mallet leaves a smoother surface, which requires less planishing. Mallets can easily be made to suit special types of work. Several standard types of mallet are shown in Fig. 2.

**Heads, Bars, Stakes, Balls, and Small Tools** (see Fig. 3).—The different shapes of heads, bars, and stakes that the coppersmith uses are too varied and numerous to illustrate.   Only the most common types are shown.   It must be remembered that the coppersmith makes his own tools to suit the individual jobs. The tools shown, however, are a part of standard coppersmithing equipment.   Various sizes of steel balls are used for bumping

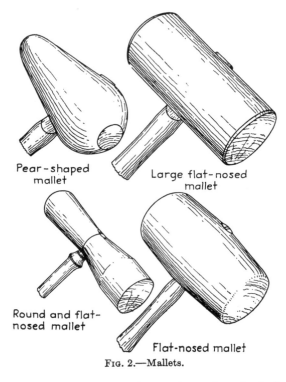

Pear-shaped mallet

Large flat-nosed mallet

Round and flat-nosed mallet

Flat-nosed mallet

Fig. 2.—Mallets.

operations.   They are usually fastened to a length of pipe or rod and then placed inside the pipe or cylinder to shape it by bumping.

**Mandrel Stand** (see Fig. 4).—The mandrel stand is a valuable piece of shop equipment and can be adapted to a variety of uses. The illustration shows the stand with two round bars.   These bars are loose in the stand and can be removed, one or the other being used as needed.   Stands are made with square openings as well as with round openings, which serve as holders for mandrels of different diameters and shapes.   The stand is made of solid cast iron, the weight being important as a counterbalance when heavy objects are hammered.

One use of the mandrel is to round or straighten a section of pipe that has been distorted or dented.   A *flatter hammer* is used, usually, when a flat surface is hammered while it lies on the mandrel.   The mandrel offers a solid backing underneath the copper being hammered, and the resulting work is smooth.

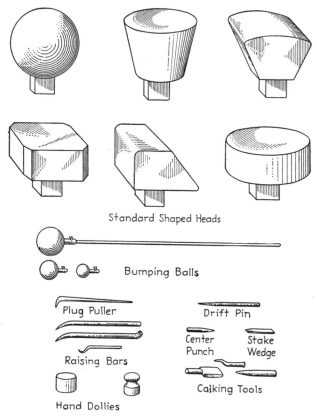

Standard Shaped Heads

Bumping Balls

Plug Puller

Drift Pin

Raising Bars

Center Punch

Stake Wedge

Calking Tools

Hand Dollies

Fig. 3.—Standard-shaped heads.

**Copper-cutting Equipment.**—Copper, being a fairly soft material, does not present difficult cutting problems.   The methods of cutting copper depend on whether it is in sheet or tube form and whether it is light or heavy gauge.

Small copper tubes may be cut with a disc roller-type tube cutter or with a hack saw.   Large pipe may be cut with a fine-tooth carpenter's saw of good steel or with a butcher's saw with a steel cutting blade, or by a metal reinforced-back cutting saw. Light sheet work is cut with tin snips; heavy sheet work can be

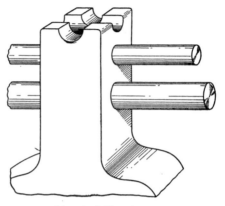

Mandrel Stand
Used for holding mandrels,
steel bars and other miscellaneous hammering equip-
ment

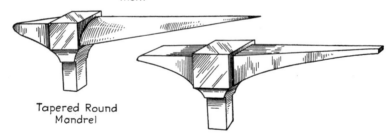

Tapered Round
Mandrel

Flat Mandrel

Fig. 4.—Mandrels.

cut with powered disc shears, with a hammer and chisel, or with a pneumatic riveting gun and a diamond-point chisel.

# CHAPTER II

## HEAT

Without a knowledge of heat and of the operation of torches, forges, and the use of wood and coke, the brazing, soldering, silver brazing, and annealing operations necessary to coppersmithing would be impossible. One of the first things for the student of coppersmithing to learn, therefore, is the operation of the different types of torches and forges. The variety of heating problems and the variety of fuels used are so great that only familiarity with the different problems and operations of individual torches and forges can teach the student how to handle each situation.

Some of the torches in use are fueled with kerosene, gasoline, manufactured or natural gas, hydrogen gas, oxyacetylene, etc. These torches throw a variety of flames for numerous uses. The large kerosene torches and natural- and manufactured-gas torches are for general work such as large brazing, annealing, and preheating, whereas the small kerosene, natural- and manufactured-gas, hydrogen, acetylene, Prestolite, and gasoline blowtorches are used in numerous coppersmithing operations ranging from tinning and wiping, spelter and bronze brazing, to steel burning.

**Kerosene Torches.**—Kerosene torches are used extensively in coppersmithing. There are two general types, pressure and vacuum. The pressure type is by far the better torch, but it is seldom used because it is dangerous. Inexperienced men often open or close the wrong valve and shoot flame 15 to 20 ft. away; there is always the danger of injuring fellow workmen and causing fires. However, when handled by careful, experienced men, the kerosene torch is a very good tool. Its best feature is its control of flame. It may be adjusted to a large, soft flame, or it may be cut down to a small and very intense flame, both of which are necessary in coppersmithing operations. A blue flame is the most efficient flame; this is adjusted by increasing the air mixture or cutting down the amount of kerosene. A white flame shows poor combustion and is a waste of fuel.

7

The most commonly used kerosene torch is the vacuum, or suction, type. This torch is made in varying sizes for large or small work.

**Gas.**—Both manufactured and natural gases are very common sources of heat in coppershops. They are used in torches and forges and are better than kerosene because there is no handling of oil and no filling of torches. The gas heat is very much like that of kerosene; but it is cleaner, more easily handled, and safer.

**Crude-oil Forges.**—Crude-oil forges are used for most flange brazing, flange preheating on large brazes, and making of tools. The crude-oil forges formerly were used in sheet brazing, but the white heat, being too blinding to look into, often resulted in brazing failure, burned copper, and poor work.

The crude-oil forges may be used on some types of annealing jobs such as short cylinders and expansion joints. This type of oil is the least expensive heat used, but it has its limitations. It radiates a blinding heat and does not respond to adjustment so readily as do other types of heat.

**Kerosene and Gas Forges.**—The kerosene and gas forges are used mostly for sheet-seam brazing when the coppersmith must be able to see into the flame to watch the brazing operation. The flame is very easily controlled, and the forge needs no preheating. It can be lighted and used immediately.

**Hydrogen Torches.**—Hydrogen gas has its special uses in coppersmithing. It is used in lead-burning and in operations where a nonoxidizing heat is necessary. Some of its other uses are for tinning, where a clean nontarnishing heat is desired, and in patching low spots on wiped flanges where more metal is needed. It is also used in loading cooking utensils with block tin. Aside from these special uses, hydrogen gas can be of general value on all small work where intense heat is necessary.

Hydrogen gas, however, is highly explosive and should be treated with great care. The tank should be kept in enclosed spaces away from heat and open flame.

Although pure hydrogen gas can be used by itself, it is usually mixed with compressed air at the torch. Mixing with air gives a more intense flame. A regulator gauge is necessary, similar to the type used on the oxygen-acetylene outfit, one gauge for the hydrogen and one for regulating the air. On hydrogen-and-air combinations, pressures ranging from 5 to 25 lb. are most generally used. When low pressures are used on the hydrogen, there is always danger of the hydrogen's igniting inside the torch tip and burning back through the hose to the gauges; if the pressure is low on the hydrogen flask, the flame may crawl into the bottle itself, causing an explosion. For this reason, a water seal is installed in the hydrogen line between the bottle and the torch outlet, so that if the fire should happen to back up into the hose, it could go only as far as the water seal.

**Gasoline Blowtorch.**—The gasoline blowtorch is a very common part of coppershop equipment. It is used on many jobs where a small soft flame is required. Some of its uses are for heating soldering irons, for doing small soldering and sweating jobs, for tinning small work, and annealing small articles. This type of torch is important because it can be taken along in a tool kit and used without much preparation and assembling.

Care must be taken not to pump too much air into it. Fewer than fifty strokes of the pump is usually the limit set for proper pumping of a quart-size torch. The safest method is to pump just enough air to produce a satisfactory blue flame. Gasoline torches should never be used without proper fire-extinguishing equipment.

**Prestolite Torch.**—Prestolite is acetylene gas furnished in small steel bottles. The torch nozzle is designed to mix its own oxygen, creating a soft blue flame. This type of heat has largely replaced the gasoline blowtorch, because it eliminates the fuel-filling hazard. When the flask is fully charged, it supplies enough heat to do small silver-brazing jobs.

The main use of Prestolite is for tinning and soldering work and for all general-purpose work where great heat is not desired. It is also convenient for use where it may be difficult to set up acetylene torches.

**Coke, Wood, and Charcoal.**—Coke is still used in many shops as the main source of heat for brazing sheet work and flanges in forges. The heat from coke is a clean heat, which can be intensified or softened by the increase or decrease of air blast. In many shops coke is used largely as backing heat for the brazing of saddle branches, cup joints, and miscellaneous work.

Charcoal is used in a manner similar to coke but has been discontinued because more efficient methods have been developed.

Charcoal is a primitive fuel and was used (and still can be used) when other, more modern, types of fuel were not available. Wood is still a very important backing for brazing, annealing, heating tin pots, and melting rosin in vats. The woodpile is still popular equipment in the coppershop and has not been supplanted by modern fuels as has charcoal.

**Acetylene.**—See Silver Brazing.

# CHAPTER III

## ANNEALING AND MELTING TEMPERATURES

The coppersmith must be acquainted with the melting points and annealing temperatures of the various metals. He must be able to recognize temperatures by their color. Color charts are merely an approximate guide, because the colors reproduced on the charts are not true to those produced in the actual working with metals. Annealing done in sunlight has an entirely different color from work of the same temperature done in a darkened place.

Although the coppersmith must be able under any condition to recognize the heat of the metal by its color, he should braze work in a slightly darkened location whenever possible. The dimness will enable the mechanic to recognize the color more easily and thus to prevent overheating while annealing or brazing.

The melting- and flow-points chart (Table I) includes most of the metals with which a coppersmith works. Both the melting points and the flow points of the metals are shown. The melting point is the sluggish state that the metal passes through in changing from a solid to a liquid condition. The flow point is that point at which the molten metal is completely liquefied and free of lumps or sluggishness.

Some metals reach the melting and the liquid states almost simultaneously, while others, especially alloys, have a variety of ranges between the melting and the flow points. Alloys such as *wiping* metal and Grades III and V, Navy Specification, silver solders have a much longer range between the melt and flow points, which is used to advantage in coppersmithing operations. Without the wide melt-flow range of wiping metal, it could never be handled as it is. The plastic state just under the flow point enables it to be wiped while the heat is adjusted to keep the metal in a mushy state.

Grades III and V, Navy Specification, silver alloys also are used advantageously on work where it is necessary to build up a fillet or where there are gaps or poor fits that must be filled up.

11

**Annealing, or Softening, Copper.**—"Annealing" means softening metals by means of a heat process. The various metals need different individual heat-treatments to anneal them. The annealing usually enables the craftsman to work or to machine the metals while cold. Copper is annealed by applying heat until the metal is cherry red; copper is fully annealed at about 1375°F. Then it may be either left to cool by itself or cooled by being dipped in water or in an acid bath. Repeated annealing of copper does not seem to affect the metal. On some jobs copper is annealed dozens of times before completion of the work.

Care should be taken that tin or solder does not come in contact with the copper when it is being annealed, because tin will burn holes through copper at annealing temperatures. Tongs and equipment sometimes have bits of tin on them, and so constant care must be exercised lest copper, brass, or bronze be spoiled. As tin and solder are parts of shop equipment, small pieces may be found anywhere throughout the shop—on forges, hooks, chains, slabs, etc.

**Annealing Brass.**—Brass, a composition of copper and zinc, is annealed by heating it to about 1000°F. and holding it there for a few minutes before letting it cool slowly. Brass should not be cooled in water. As there are many different grades of brass, there is a wide range of melting points due to the varying proportions of copper and zinc.

**Annealing Copper-nickel Alloy.**—Copper-nickel pipe is usually annealed at the factory before it is shipped. It should be worked as much as possible before further annealing. If further annealing is necessary, the copper-nickel alloy should be brought to about 1450°F. and held at that temperature for a few minutes, then allowed to cool by itself. This annealing is not as good as the factory annealing, but it serves the purpose for the coppersmith.

**Annealing Composition *F*, Navy Specifications.**—Spelter-brazing flanges and fittings are made of composition *F* alloy, which melts at 1796°F., allowing about 175°F. as a safety factor above that of spelter. The annealing of this metal is similar to the method used in annealing brass; however, annealing of composition *F* is not necessary because the composition itself is not worked or ever intended to be worked. This is also true of composition *M*.

# TABLE I.—MELTING- AND FLOW-POINTS CHART

| Metal | Melt point | Flow point | Copper | Iron | Lead | Manganese | Nickel | Silicon | Tin | Zinc |
|---|---|---|---|---|---|---|---|---|---|---|
| Aluminum | 1220 | | | | | | | | | |
| Borax | 1330 | | | | | | | | | |
| Brass, navy roll | 1545 | | 59. 61. | .10 | .20 | | | | | *R |
| Brass spelter Grade A | 1621 | | 49. 52. | .10 | .50 | | | | | R |
| Grade B | 1652 | | 49. 52. | .10 | .50 | | | | 3. 4. | R |
| Grade C | 1724 | | 68. 72. | .10 | .30 | | | | | R |
| Grade D | 1800 | | 78. 82. | .10 | .20 | | | | | R |
| Bronze, Everdure | 1832 | | R | .75 | | | | 10. 12. | .25 | .25 |
| Bronze, Tobin | 1625 | | | | | | | | | |
| Cadmium | 610 | | | | | | | | | |
| Composition F | 1796 | | 85. | | | | | | | 15. |
| Composition M | About 1750 | | 86.5 91.0 | 0.15 | 1.0 2.0 | | 1. | | 5.5 6.5 | 1.5 5.0 |
| Copper | 1981 | | | | | | | | | |
| Copper nickel | 2200 | | R | .30 .50 | .05 | .50 1.0 | 29. 32. | | 1.20 | 1.0 |
| Flux, silver brazing | 800 | 1100 | | | | | | | | |
| Iron | 2785 | | | | | | | | | |
| Lead | 621 | | | | | | | | | |
| Monel | 2460 | | R | 2.5 | | 2.0 | 63. 70. | .5 | | |
| Nickel | 2646 | | | | | | | | | |
| Rosin | 200 | | | | | | | | | |
| Silver | 1762 | | | | | | | | | |
| Solder ½ × ½ Grade A | 360 | 415 | | | R | | | | 49. | |
| Grade B | 360 | 440 | | | R | | | | 44. | |
| Grade C | 360 | 465 | | | R | | | | 38. | |
| Wiping metal Grade D | 370 | 430 | | | R | | | | 35. | |
| Grade E | 370 | 460 | | | R | | | | 30. | |
| Grade F | 330 | 355 | | | R | | | | 70. | |
| Solder paste | 120 (approx.) | | | | | | | | | |
| Tallow | 114 | | | | | | | | | |
| Tin | 449 | | | | | | | | | |
| Zinc | 787 | | | | | | | | | |

* Remainder.

**Composition *M*, Navy Specifications.**—Silver-brazing flanges and silver-solder fittings are made of composition *M*, melting at approximately 1750°F. It is designed for silver-braze fittings and may be annealed in the same manner as is brass.

**Annealing Lead.**—Lead is annealed either with steam or with heat from a soft flame. When annealed, it is warm and does not show any change of color. For this reason, and because the melting point is quite low, 621°F., annealing it with a torch is a very uncertain and tricky operation. When annealing lead with a torch, adjust to a soft flame and then play it on the part that is to be annealed. Keep the torch moving, and after each rotation of the torch, feel the lead to determine the warmth. When it becomes a little too hot for hand comfort, it is sufficiently annealed.

# CHAPTER IV

## ACIDS

Without acids a great many coppersmithing operations would· be very difficult, if not impossible. Acid is used principally for cleaning metals. No mysterious action occurs when metals are being cleaned with acids. The acids merely dissolve and remove the oxides from the metals. The metals could, in most cases, be cleaned just as thoroughly by mechanical means, but acid is more convenient because it can be used as a bath, the metals being immersed while they are hot or cold, depending on the type of acid used. Piping and various fittings would be very difficult to clean, especially inside, by mechanical methods. For them the acid bath is best. Also, the use of acids results in a cleaner, more workmanlike product.

Dating back to the earliest known periods, acids originally were ordinary salt brine and animal and human urine. These acids were effective, if not pleasant, to use. Acids in modern use are sulphuric, which is usually diluted, muriatic (hydrochloric), and nitric.

Acid vats are made of wood and are lead lined, then lined again with wood to protect the soft lead lining from being punctured by the metals being immersed. Acids should be handled in lead or glass containers, and special acid goggles should be worn at all times when one is handling or working with acids. On jobs where the workman has to work with acid continuously for hours at a time, the use of rubber gloves and aprons is advisable, as the acid will injure the skin and ruin clothing.

Acids should not be allowed to remain on metal once the job is completed. Copper and nonferrous (containing no iron) metals will turn green (develop verdigris), and ferrous metals will rust. For this reason, all traces of acids must be neutralized by being washed off with fresh water, and on completion the work should be thoroughly dried.

**Sulphuric Acid.**—Sulphuric acid is used for general cleaning of copper, brass, bronze, etc. It is mixed in the proportion of 1

15

part acid to 10 parts water. The water being mixed is poured into the vat or container; then the acid is added. **Never pour water into acid, for it will cause a violent action or explosion. The acid should always be added to the water.** Acid cleans better when metals are hot. The dip, or immersion, method is the best if proper equipment is available. Swabbing with acid is done when the work is too large for dipping. The metal should be warm for best results, the swabbing being done with old brooms or swabs made of waste or woollen materials.

The practice of dipping copper into acid while copper is red-hot has been, and is being, done by many coppersmiths. This practice is unnecessary and dangerous. After annealing, the copper should be left to cool, at least until the color leaves it, before being dipped into the acid. The fumes and spray from red-hot copper pipe may injure clothing or workmen. **An accidental spray of acid in the eyes should be washed out immediately with cold water. Then, if further treatment is needed, a doctor should be consulted. When handling acid, workmen should always wear goggles.**

**Procedure for Cleaning Copper with Sulphuric Acid.**—Apply heat to about 500°F., or anneal, dip in acid, and remove. Wash the metal with clean cold water, scour with fine sand, wash again with water, and then dry with a torch.

**Muriatic (Hydrochloric) Acid.**—Muriatic acid is used full strength in most coppersmithing operations. It is used largely for cleaning copper, brass, bronze, steel, and castings for tinning.

Muriatic acid is also used to clean copper-nickel alloy. For best results, the copper nickel should be warmed to about 300°F. and then dipped into a vat, but this procedure is discouraged because of the weakening effect of heat on muriatic acid. Therefore, when muriatic acid is being used for cleaning, the metals are usually dipped cold.

**Cut or Killed Acid (Zinc Chloride).**—Cut acid is used as a flux for tinning or soldering. It is made by putting zinc into fresh muriatic acid, thereby causing a violent boiling action. The acid is cut when additional zinc causes no further action.

**Removing Salt Deposits from the Interior of Pipes.**—Brine lines on evaporators develop a coating of salt. This coating becomes thicker with time and eventually, if not removed, clogs the pipe completely. These salt deposits are removed by the following method:

Heat the complete length of the pipe slowly with a torch until it is thoroughly warm, about 200°F., then plunge it in cold water. Care should be taken to see that the pipe is not heated enough to melt tin or wiping metal. Bolt on testing blanks, subject pipe to about 100-lb. water pressure, then hammer full length of pipe with flatter or planishing hammer. Remove blanks and shake out salt lumps. The remaining salt may be removed by soaking the pipe in muriatic acid. The complete desalting job can be done with muriatic acid, but the acid is useless for any other purpose after once being used this way. As a rule the piping used on salt-water lines is either tinned or tinned and wiped. Therefore, if acid is used in removing salt deposits, the pipe must be retinned or rewiped.

**Nitric Acid.**—Nitric acid is used for special cleaning purposes when a powerful cleaner is desired. This acid is not used very much because inexperienced mechanics pour nitric acid into the muriatic vat, thus mixing muriatic with nitric acid. This combination has a strong action on brass, and, if castings were left too long in this bath, they would be partially or completely dissolved.

**Cleaning Hydraulic Piping.**—Hydraulic oil piping used on modern naval guns must be cleaned with meticulous care to prevent any small particle of foreign matter from entering the delicate machinery. For this reason, a special method of cleaning is required.

The first step of the process used in cleaning this hydraulic piping is to apply paraffin to all steel or iron flanges or unions. The paraffin will prevent the acid from corroding the ferrous metals. After applying paraffin to all ferrous metals, clean the pipe by dipping it into a bath of special acid composed of 1 part nitric, 2 parts sulphuric acid, and 4 parts water. Let it remain in the acid until clean. When clean, remove the piping from the acid, wash it with water, and then neutralize it in a bath of 1½ lb. potash to 1 gal. water. This is an instantaneous dip. Wash with water again, and then apply steam along the complete length of the pipe, inside and out, to remove whatever foreign matter may be lodged in the pipe and at the same time to dry it.

The paraffin will also be removed by this steam bath.   Then cover the ends with lintproof rags or canvas.

**Cleaning    Lubricating-oil    Piping.**—Lubricating-oil    piping aboard modern ships is usually made of copper.   This piping must, of course, be free of dirt, and all trace of acid must be removed before installation.   The method of cleaning "lub-oil" piping is to dip it thoroughly in sulphuric acid and then to wash it with water.   The acid is then neutralized by washing the pipe in a 20-min. bath of a hot solution composed of 1 lb. soda ash to $6\frac{3}{4}$ gal. water.   This solution removes all trace of acid from the copper.   After removing from the neutralizing bath, steam the pipe thoroughly, blowing out foreign matter and drying the pipe in one operation.   Cover ends with lintproof rags or canvas.

# CHAPTER V

## TINNING AND THE USE OF SOLDERS

In the ordinary mechanic's language, "soldering" is considered the joining together of metals with a tin-lead alloy, commonly called "half and half," that melts at about 365 to 400°F. The coppersmith, however, broadens the term to "hard" solders and "soft" solders. "Hard" denotes a solder with a melting point above 1000°F. and "soft" indicates a point below 1000°F. Some authorities establish a dividing line at 1000°F., with joinings completed below that temperature termed "soldering" and those above termed "brazing," such as "spelter brazing" and "silver brazing." Since the use of the terms differs according to individual preference, it is important that the mechanic understand their broadness. In most shops "soldering" is classified as the use of tin-lead combinations, and "brazing" as the use of spelter (copper-zinc) and silver-alloy combinations with melting temperatures above 1000°F.

**Solders.**—Starting with the lower-melting-point solders, first is the 2-part-tin, 1-part-lead solder, which melts at 330°F. and flows at 355°F. The next is half-and-half solder, which melts at 360°F. and flows at 415°F. This combination is most commonly used because it is the cheapest high-grade solder with a low melting point.

Wiping solder (about 2 parts lead and 1 part tin) is used for coating the inside of salt-water piping and castings to protect them from being corroded by salt-water action. Wiping solder has a long melting-flowing range, melting at 370°F. and flowing at 430°F. This long range enables the metal to be worked while being heated, much the same as plaster.

**Tinning.**—In coppersmithing, tinning is one of the most important uses of solder. Any of the tin-lead combinations may be used for tinning, or pure block tin alone may be used.

"Tinning" is the process of applying a coating of tin or solder to other metals by the use of heat and fluxes. This is accomplished in various ways, such as by dipping or by the hand method of tinning. In the dipping method, the article is immersed in a molten tin bath. A layer of scum forms on the top of tin after it is melted in a pot; before dip tinning it should be removed by sprinkling powdered rosin or some tallow on the surface, then stirring the tin. The scum can then be easily removed with a suitable paddle or ladle because the scum gathers together. This leaves the surface clean and slick for dip tinning.

**Soft Solders.**—Pewter cannot be soldered with ordinary half-and-half solders because it is generally softer than the solder itself, a fact that causes holes to be melted in the pewter. For this reason low-melting-point solders are necessary. The following is a list of solders recommended by *Letter Circular* LC-493 issued by the National Bureau of Standards, Washington, D.C.:

| Lead, Per Cent | Tin, Per Cent | Bismuth, Per Cent |
|---|---|---|
| 25 | 25 | 50 |
| 50 | 35.5 | 12.5 |
| 25 | 50 | 25 |

**Other Soft Solders.**—Melting point about 450°F.:

| Tin, Per Cent | Antimony, Per Cent |
|---|---|
| 95 | 5 |

**High-melting-point Soft Solder.**—Melting point about 640°F.:

| Cadmium, Per Cent | Silver, Per Cent |
|---|---|
| 95 | 5 |

**Fluxes.**—An excellent flux for soft soldering and tinning is a mixture of ammonium chloride and zinc chloride. Proportions by weight are

| Zinc Chloride, Per Cent | Ammonium Chloride, Per Cent |
|---|---|
| 71 | 29 |

**Tinning a Copper Pipe by the Dip Method.**—Clean the pipe with acid, scrub with wire brush or sand, and then, if necessary, scrape with file or scraper to make sure that the copper is perfectly clean. Apply cut acid thoroughly and then dip the pipe into the tinning vat. The dipping should be done slowly so that the tin will not splatter. If tin splatters, lift the pipe from the vat and place it in again slowly. When the pipe is completely immersed, let it lie for a while in order to warm it through.

Then remove it and examine closely for dirty spots. If dirty spots are found, clean them with a file or scraper, apply cut acid, and dip into vat again. When completely tinned, the surplus tin should be wiped off with waste or rags.

**Safety.**—Care should be taken to avoid air pockets when dipping pipe or fittings into the molten metal. The air pockets may cause an explosion, spraying hot molten metal with a violent force and injuring workmen.

**Tinning Copper Pipe by the Hand Method.**—The cleaning is similar to any method of cleaning copper for tinning, except that, if the job is too large for dip cleaning, it may be swabbed first, while the metal is hot, with sulphuric acid; then, if a stronger cleaning agent is desired, muriatic acid may be used.

When the pipe is clean, apply cut acid and sprinkle powdered tin or use bar solder. Half-and-half solder is best unless pure tin is specified. Apply heat, moving the torch so that a large area will be heated. When the pipe is hot enough to melt tin, the tin should be rubbed with a rag or with waste that has been dipped in sal ammoniac. This procedure is followed until the pipe is completely tinned.

Small surfaces of small articles or thin-gauge metals may be tinned with a copper soldering iron, the heat for the tinning being supplied by the soldering iron  The soldering iron itself should be tinned at the tip before it is used for tinning. The soldering iron may be heated with any available heat, such as a wood fire, a blowtorch, a forge, etc. The fluxes for tinning the soldering irons themselves may be sal ammoniac, cut acid, or various solder fluxes. The method used for tinning with the soldering iron is to clean the surface to be tinned, apply flux, lay the hot soldering iron on the surface until it heats, place a little bar solder on the iron, and rub the melted solder onto the surface with the iron until the solder sticks.

**Burned Tin.**—If too much heat is applied during tinning, the tin turns a golden-yellow color, the coppersmith's gauge for burned tin. This is an undesirable result, and the work should be retinned. Retinning is the same as tinning; the work is cleaned, heated, and fluxed as usual. A completely burned tin job will turn black.

Tin can also be burned while it is being heated in the pot. When heating the pot of tin, reduce the heat as soon as the tin starts to break down. Stirring will help to melt the tin. If tin is overheated in the pot, a thick scum will form on the surface of the molten tin. This scum is merely wasted metal and cannot be used. It must be skimmed off and discarded.

**Pure Tin** (**Block Tin**).—Copper food containers and cooking utensils are covered inside and sometimes outside with a coating of pure tin, called "block tin." The color of pure tin is brighter and has a more shining appearance than that of solder. A bar of pure tin has a "sing," or crackle, to it while it is being bent.

**Powdered Tin and Solder.**—Powdered tin or powdered solder is frequently used to facilitate tinning jobs. The powdering is done by pouring molten metal into a cupped piece of canvas, closing the end like a sack, and shaking and pounding the sack until the metal cools. When cool, the metal is powdered. Sometimes the tin or solder is screened and only the fine powder is used. The rest may be reused.

**Soldering and Tinning Fluxes.**—Cut acid is the most common flux used for tinning and soldering. There are many patented fluxes on the market, some of which are very good for use on steel, monel, stainless steel, and copper-nickel alloy.

*Soldering paste* is usually of a petrolatum, wax, and rosin base and is noncorrosive. It is valuable for work where water cannot be used for washing, such as in electrical work and small jobs.

**Wiping with Solder or Wiping Metal.**—In marine work, wiping metal is used to prevent the action of salt water and electricity from eating holes in pipe. This action is called "electrolysis," or "galvanic action."

Another name for wiping metal is Grade D solder. Its composition is 2 parts lead to 1 part tin. Wiping metal is sometimes "doctored," or remixed, by adding more lead or tin. This is done usually by inexperienced mechanics who have difficulty in handling or wiping the metal. This practice is unnecessary because wiping metal, when it comes in the original bars, is mixed in the proper proportions. Tallow is used as a flux.

The method of applying this metal is called "wiping." The pipe must first be tinned, then washed with water so as to remove all acid flux. Set up the pipe so that it has a slight downhill fall toward you. Get all necessary equipment ready, such as wiping pads, wiping sticks, and tallow. Have wiping metal ready and molten in a pot near by. Heat the pipe with a torch on the bottom and sides at the middle section; when the metal is slightly warm, apply tallow. Dip into the wiping-metal pot with a ladle that has been previously heated, stirring the metal thoroughly. Dip from the bottom of the pot and not from the top. Dip out the metal and pour it into the pipe, on the bottom, and on the sides. Have wiping cloth or stick in one hand and torch in the other; heat the pipe from the outside until the wiping metal can be handled like soft putty. Wipe the metal where desired, keeping an even thickness not less than $\frac{1}{16}$ in. Keep wiping all surplus metal toward yourself, heating where heat is needed and adding more wiping metal when necessary. If wiping metal is reheated several times in the pipe, the tin will separate from the lead and come to the surface, sticking to the wiping cloth and making it impossible to do good work. In such a case as this, it is advisable to remove all metal from the pipe, place it in the pot, remelt it, and stir together again.

When melted in a pot, the wiping metal should be stirred before each ladling. The tin rises to the surface and separates from the lead, and the stirring will keep the proportion more even while the wiping metal is being used.

**Cleaning Old Castings for Tinning.**—Cast tees, ells, and spools occasionally develop leaks when in service, and many times these leaks may be repaired by dip tinning.

Cleaning old castings for tinning is difficult sometimes because of the porous nature of cast metal. The thickness of the casting is sometimes honeycombed with small air pockets, and thoroughly cleaning these small pockets is practically impossible. The method of cleaning is to warm the casting very slowly with a soft heat or a wood fire to remove moisture and excess grease from the pores. (**Caution: Do not heat quickly with an intense heat.** This may generate steam in the pores and break the casting.)

When the casting is warmed through, it should be cleaned with a wire brush, to remove paint and scale, and then dipped into the muriatic acid bath. While it is in the acid bath, it should be wire brushed and scraped to remove all foreign substances. When all visible dirt is removed and the casting clean and bright, it should be fluxed with cut acid and then dip tinned in the tinning vat. The casting is tinned by lowering it slowly into the molten tin and letting it submerge completely. When bubbles no longer appear at the surface of the tin, remove the casting and

inspect it for dirty spots.  If still dirty, reclean and retin.
**(Caution: Do not pour molten metal on cold wet surface because it will splatter dangerously.)**

**Porous Flanges and Castings.**—Castings are often porous, and the coppersmith, after finding the leaks, must make them tight. There are three general methods of taking care of leaks in porous flanges.  They are the silver-brazing method, the tinning (either dip tinning or hand tinning), and the calking method, which is not recommended unless the other methods cannot be used.

In the silver-brazing method, the leaks in castings are flooded, or tinned, with a coating of silver solder.  The area surrounding the leak should also be silver brazed.  The tinning method is used when the complete casting is porous and silver brazing would be too expensive and difficult.  The dip method of tinning is the best whenever the necessary facilities are available. However, hand tinning is often used (see Hand Tinning, page 21). The calking method is used but not recommended.  Calking tools are used to tap the holes shut.

**Sweating Together Threaded Joints** (see Fig. 5).—Threaded pipe that is to be used on air, oil, or gas installations should be, whenever practicable, tinned and sweated together to ensure leakproof connections.  "Sweating" is joining tinned parts together so that the tin from both parts melts into a solid joint and, when cool, holds the parts rigidly together.  Copper, brass, bronze, or steel can be sweated this way.

The procedure in tinning and sweating is to clean the threads well and then to tin them.  Do not be careless while tinning since it is the most important operation.  After both parts of the joint have been tinned, wash them with clean water, apply flux, and then reheat.  Reheat both parts and then screw them together, adding the solder.  Keep enough heat on the joint so that the solder does not get cold and harden while the parts are being screwed together.  When they are screwed together tightly, add enough solder to make a full bead on the surface of the shoulder.  If pinholes show on the surface bead, reheat and add flux.  Never allow a job to pass if it has pinholes showing; every pinhole is a potential leak.

Tinning and sweating are especially worth while when old screwed fittings have to be used again.  Old threads should be

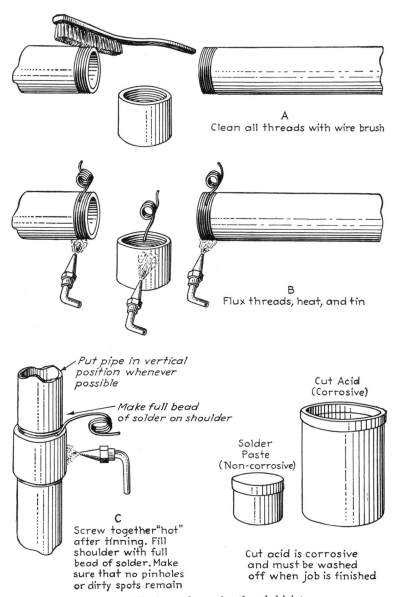

FIG. 5.—Tinning and sweating threaded joints.

cleaned first with muriatic acid. An ordinary blowtorch is sufficient heat for tinning and sweating operations.

Disassembling may be done by reheating and unscrewing. Cut-acid flux is most commonly used, but it must be washed off or it will tarnish the work. Noncorrosive solder paste may be used as a flux wherever the washing cannot be done.

**Stripping Solder or Tin from Copper or Brass.**—Stripping the tin from a pipe is necessary when spelter brazing or silver brazing is to be done on piping that has been tinned. This is usually done when tinned pipes are to be repaired. First the pipe is heated and *dry wiped*. The term "to dry wipe" means to remove all lumps and surplus tin from the pipe while the pipe is hot enough to melt the tin. This is done by wiping it with a rag or waste. All surplus lumps must be removed from both the inside and the outside of the pipe; care must be taken so that the tin is not burned into the pipe by excessive heating. Excessive heating will turn the tin a golden color and will cause it to burn into the copper, pitting the copper or burning holes through it.

After all the surplus tin has been removed, the pipe is cooled in water. When the pipe is cool, the *stripping mixture* is applied. The proportions of the stripping mixture are 1 part sal ammoniac (ammonium chloride) to 10 parts fire clay; add enough fresh muriatic acid (hydrochloric) to make a sloppy mixture and stir thoroughly. Apply the stripping mixture to the whole pipe with rag or waste; swab the mixture on the inside and outside as thickly as possible. Then place the pipe on the annealing tables. Anneal thoroughly. When the pipe has been annealed, brush off the stripping mixture with a wire brush and then douse the pipe in a sulphuric bath. Remove from the sulphuric bath, wash with water, and examine to see how thoroughly the tin has been removed.

If some tin still remains, the pipe should be swabbed again with the stripping mixture, reannealed, doused in acid, and washed. The second application usually strips a pipe clean of tin.

# CHAPTER VI

## BRAZING

Brazing is joining together by means of alloys other metals that have a higher melting point. It is one of the most important skills of the coppersmithing trade. The actual brazing is not difficult to understand, but the setup for brazing and the laying up of the work should not be underestimated by the coppersmith. The laying up of metals preparatory to brazing, the cleaning, the fluxes, the spelters, the silver alloys, and the brazing setup are points that require careful consideration and study. The problems concerned in brazing are many, and no attempt is being made to cover the entire art. In coppersmithing, the most common brazing jobs are flanges, branches, bosses, cup joints, and sheets. The two main types of brazes are spelter brazes and silver brazes, although anything above 1000°F. is considered brazing.

**Spelter Brazing.**—In many coppersmithing operations, spelter brazing is preferred to silver brazing for various reasons. The most common is that copper pipes or sheets are formed after being brazed, and to do this forming, it is necessary to anneal the copper between workings. This annealing would be impossible to do if the sheets were silver brazed, because silver solder melts at 1300°F. The silver would melt while the copper was being annealed. Many times it is necessary to make two brazes very close to each other. At such times, if both brazes cannot be done at once, it is advantageous to braze the first joint with spelter, which has the higher melting point, and the second with silver.

Spelter is also much cheaper than silver, and, when cost must be considered, it is more economical to use.

**Spelter.**—Spelter is a composition of copper and zinc. The most commonly used spelter is the 50% copper-50% zinc composition, melting at approximately 1620°F. Spelter is often used in the grain form because of ease in handling. On most of the large coppersmithing jobs, the brazing setup is such that spelter in the rod form would be unsatisfactory. The heat is so great that the coppersmith could not get near enough to the work to apply the spelter in the rod form.

**Seam Spelter.**—Higher melting point spelters, melting up to 1775°F., are sometimes used on sheet-seam work. This spelter is not used much, because of the danger of melting the copper. The short range between the melting point of the copper and the melting temperature of this spelter necessitates great skill in handling in order to prevent the copper from melting during the braze. The lower melting spelter is the more practical for all-round work. Ordinary 50% copper-50% zinc spelter is successful on most jobs, but for sheet work that must be hammered or worked considerably, the seam spelter is recommended, because its higher percentage of copper, about 80 per cent, makes it a very ductile metal, able to withstand severe hammering before it tears or breaks. It can also be worked while hot.

**Fine- and Coarse-grain Spelter.**—Spelter usually is manufactured in different sizes or grains, and, although the composition is the same, the action is different, depending on the work it is used for. The fine-grain spelter is best for small, thin-gauge, sheet work. The coarse-grain spelter is best for general-purpose larger work. Fine-grain spelter is not very satisfactory in large work, because its action, during brazing, is different from coarse grain. The smaller pieces offer more surface to oxidation and need more borax to counteract it, but even then the action is very sluggish and often leaves a rough job. This action occurs only when large work is being brazed and large amounts of fine spelter are used. On small thin-sheet work, where very little spelter is used, the fine-grain spelter works very well.

Large-grain spelter, $\frac{1}{8}$ to $\frac{1}{4}$ in. thick, is used generally and can be used even on small work if reasonable care is taken while the metal is being brazed.

**Welding Rods.**—Welding rods made of bronze and special alloys are used commonly throughout the coppersmithing trade. Their melting points are similar to spelters; in fact they are merely spelters in a more convenient form. These rods are used most in connection with the acetylene torch and are said to yield results more quickly than ordinary spelter brazing. They compare with silver solder in the same manner that spelter does.

Even with the so-called "speed methods" of using bronze rods for brazing, they are not very popular with coppersmiths because the intense heat of the acetylene torch is likely to sear or burn the copper at or near the point of the braze, thus creating a weak spot that will give way under vibration or stress. However, the practice of using acetylene and bronze rod is standard in many shops, and in the hands of a highly skilled coppersmith the results can be very satisfactory.

**Steps Preparatory to Spelter Brazing.**—Clean the work thoroughly. With a solution of water and borax (about 1 table-spoon or more of borax to a cup of clean water), flux the parts to be joined. This solution is usually mixed with spelter and is kept handy on the job. Care must be taken that oil, grease, solder, or foreign matter is not placed on the part that is to be brazed.

**Equipment.**—Pokers and bars are used in brazing in order to aid and control the flow of spelter and to lay together again metals that have spread apart from heat expansion. These pokers and bars should be free from tin or solder before being used for brazing.

**Removing Wires.**—Wires that are necessary to hold work together for brazing are sometimes brazed solidly to the work. These wires, if removed while work is still red-hot, will come off easily, but, if the work is allowed to cool before they are removed, the metal itself may be torn away with the wire. The best rule, especially when the brazed metal is very thin, is to reheat the work to an annealing heat and remove the wire while the work is red-hot.

**Penetration.**—The penetration of solder into the metals being brazed is largely determined by the melting point of the solder being used. Low-melting tin and lead solders have a superficial penetration when applied, because the pores open very little during tinning. During silver brazing or spelter brazing, how-ever, the penetration is deeper because the higher temperature necessary to melt these brazing solders opens the pores con-siderably more, allowing for deeper penetration. If the heating is improperly done, the penetration is poor, resulting in weak joints and leaks. Every effort should be made to get the fullest penetration possible for the type of solder being used and still to avoid burning the metals being brazed.

**Cold Brazing.**—"Cold braze" is a term given to a braze that has been insufficiently heated, the penetration being poor and superficial. Sometimes a job appears to be well brazed, but when it is tested or hammered, flaws or leaks show. This failure may sometimes be traced to several things: a poor setup, improper distribution of heat, inexperience, or carelessness. The remedy, of course, is re-brazing.

**Pinholes.**—During brazing or soldering, it often happens that pinholes are visible in the braze after it has been made. In this case, it is best to reheat the job, add more flux, and remelt the part that shows the pinholes. Usually a thorough re-brazing will eliminate them. The pinholes may be caused by underheating or by dirt particles that remained in the braze and did not boil to the surface during brazing.

**Drafts.**—During brazing operations, doors and windows should be closed to prevent drafts upon the work or workmen. There are two reasons why it is advisable to prevent drafts, especially on large brazing work: first, it is difficult to heat the work evenly when the flames are fanned by drafts, and, second, the extreme contrast of the chill draft behind and the high temperature of the braze in front causes great physical discomfort to the workmen.

**Silver Solders.**—Silver solders are made in six grades, 0 to V, three of which are in general use in marine shipbuilding. The three grades used are Grades III, IV, and V.

Grade III is used on nearly all nonferrous silver-brazing work, brass, bronze, and other copper-base alloys (except copper-nickel branch work or stainless steel, which is best handled with Grades IV or V). Grade III has a low silver content, with quite a low flow point, 1300°F., and thus can easily be used on nearly all low-melting yellow brass.

Grade IV silver solder is designed for ferrous work, nickel-copper, steel, and stainless-steel combinations. It flows at 1175°F.

Grade V silver solder has somewhat the same use as Grade IV, except that it can be used more easily in work where gaps must be filled. Because of the comparatively long melting-flowing range, it can be used as a filler when fits are loose and sloppy.

Silver solder for ordinary use can be made from soft brass and silver, 2 parts brass to 1 part silver.

**Cleaning.**—The work should first be cleaned with the best possible means available. Acid or manual methods may be used. On most work it is best if both are used, first the acid, then wire brushing, scraping, filing, or sandpapering until the metals to be brazed shine brightly.

TABLE II.—SILVER-SOLDER MIXTURES AND MELT AND FLOW POINTS
(Taken from *Letter Circular* LC-493, National Bureau of Standards, Washington, D.C.)

| Color | Silver | Copper | Zinc | Melt point, °F. | Flow point, °F. |
|---|---|---|---|---|---|
| Yellow................. | 10 | 52 | 38 | 1510 | 1600 |
| Yellow................. | 20 | 45 | 35 | 1430 | 1500 |
| Nearly white............. | 45 | 30 | 25 | 1250 | 1370 |
| Nearly white..... ...... | 50 | 34 | 16 | 1280 | 1425 |
| White ................. | 65 | 20 | 15 | 1280 | 1325 |
| White................. | 70 | 20 | 10 | 1335 | 1390 |
| White................. | 80 | 16 | 4 | 1360 | 1460 |

**General Outline and Procedure of Silver Brazing.**—Clean the parts to be brazed. Remove all dirt and discoloration. If the parts are covered with grease or oil, remove it by heat; burn it off, clean with acid, and then scrape with scraper or wire brush until the metal shines brightly. **Do not attempt to braze dirty metals.**

When metals are clean, flux should be applied with a brush to the area that is to be brazed. Sometimes flux is added to surrounding parts to aid in cleaning after brazing.

Make all work fit snugly before brazing. Be sure to secure work solidly before beginning to braze. Select the proper-sized torch and begin heating the work. When the flux begins to melt and the work becomes a dark red, apply the silver. Do not melt the silver directly with the torch flame as the silver should be melted by the heat of the work. When the job has been brazed and is about hand cool, it may be cleaned with wire brush and water.

**Disassembling Silver-soldered Joints.**—Heat the work completely on the circumference until the silver solder melts, and then pull the joints apart. Care must be taken when disassembling brass castings, because they become brittle when heated. Do not rock or twist them too much when pulling them apart, as you may spread the opening of the fitting or crack it at the brazing collar. When fittings are pulled apart, they should be reheated and the excess silver, while molten, removed with a wire brush. **Never hammer on silver solder fittings while they are hot.**

**Cleaning Silver-brazed Fittings after Brazing.**—Silver-brazed fittings and pipe may be cleaned either with acid or with warm water and a wire brush. Acid is the best method if the work is being done in the shop where acid-bath facilities are available. Because it is impractical to use acid for cleaning purposes aboard ship, scrub the fitting with a wire brush and water while the metal is still warm.

**Silver-inserted Fittings.**—Fittings with a silver-solder band inserted in the connecting ends are now used extensively, instead of threaded or spelter-brazed fittings, in the shipbuilding industry for making pipe connections. These fittings simplify the installation of pipe systems on copper, brass, and copper-nickel lines because they are easier to install. Men can be trained more quickly to make leakproof piping systems with silver-brazed or silver-insert fittings than by the older pipe-threading or spelter-brazing methods.

Theoretically, there is enough silver solder in the fittings to make a perfect joint, but in practice it is often advisable to add a little silver solder to the fittings in order to play safe, especially if a job is situated where it would be difficult to re-braze in case it leaked. Of course, the practice of adding silver solder to joints may be carried too far, and silver wasted. A very common erroneous practice, when silver brazing, is to build a large, high surface bead of silver solder at the collar of the fitting. This surface silver is not necessary if the joint is brazed correctly.

**Silver Brazing a Flange.**—Cut the pipe ends square, file away all burrs and unevenness, and clean the pipe and flange with acids or by mechanical methods. Apply flux to both flange and pipe, fluxing only the parts to be brazed.

Apply heat at the collar of the flange with a circular motion; play the heat onto the pipe, heating it but concentrating it on the flange, since it is the heavier of the two metals. Both parts should be brought to the brazing heat simultaneously.

When the work becomes dark red, or when the flux is flowing freely, place the silver solder at the flange collar shoulder, where most of the heat is concentrated. Keep moving the torch as the solder melts, until sufficient solder is flowed onto the work to make a smooth bead. Continue this procedure until the flange is brazed completely.

Draw the silver to the full depth of the socket. Always file the face of the flange slightly after silver brazing because particles of silver or flux fastened to the face will prevent making a tight joint.

**Oxidation.**—Oxide is the scale that forms on metals, causing flaking and rust. Copper scales off after annealing, and this scale is copper oxide. Metals also oxidize through exposure to air. After copper has been cleaned thoroughly and then is exposed to air for any length of time, it will gradually become dull in appearance; the luster leaves it as a result of oxidation.

This oxide must be removed before the metal is brazed. During brazing or soldering operations, some agent must be used to keep this oxidation down, and this is done by the use of various fluxes. The fluxes cover the surface and prevent the air from causing oxidation, and they also dissolve whatever oxides are formed, keeping a surface clean for fusing. They also serve as a conductor of heat to the spelter or silver alloys.

**Fluxes.**—A flux of some sort is always used to increase the fusing and flow of metals being brazed or soldered. No matter what metals are being joined, all fluxes have a similar purpose, namely, control of oxidation.

Borax is used for high-temperature brazing from about 1350 to 1800°F. A patented commercial flux is used on most silver-solder work in low-temperature brazing. It is intended for work from about 1100 to 1300°F. Heat causes borax to swell, thus making it rise slightly from the work, especially when large amounts of borax are used. This is a natural action caused by the heat at a certain temperature. When the temperature rises to about 1300°F., the borax melts and clings to the metal in a sticky liquid state. At this stage the borax is active, keeping the metal clean by dissolving oxides that are formed by the heat. As the temperature rises to the melting heat of spelter, the spelter flows into the pores of the metal that have been kept clean by the borax flux. Borax in the lump form is kept on hand and is broken or ground in a small iron mortar as needed. Powdered borax is available commercially, but it is not recommended because it becomes "air slacked," or dirty, from exposure to air and is less effective than freshly ground borax.

**Silver-brazing Flux.**—Patented commercial silver-solder flux is recommended for all silver brazing. It should be mixed with clean water to a creamy consistency and should be applied to the work with a brush. **(Caution: This flux is injurious and should never be applied with the fingers.)** It melts at about 800°F. and is completely liquid at 1100°F. The action of the flux can be used as a temperature guide, especially in bright sunlight, where it is difficult to determine the color of the heated metal. All fluxes should be applied to the work before the work is heated.

**Overheating Effects on Flux (Silver Brazing).**—While a workman is silver brazing, especially when silver brazing copper-nickel, stainless steels, or steel, the effects of overheating can be very confusing and may result in brazing failure. Many silver-brazing failures are caused by too much heat being applied to a braze, thus burning away the flux, leaving none to dissolve or counteract the oxide as it forms. This creates a condition similar to brazing without any flux. The condition is more pronounced when copper-nickel alloy, stainless steels, or steel is being brazed.

Applying the flux in a thick paste form helps to prevent this condition from appearing on the metals. Apply the heat, whenever possible, to the section away from flux, letting the work become heated from adjoining parts. This prevents excess heat from getting to the section that is being brazed.

**Corrosive Action of Silver-solder Flux.**—Silver-solder flux has a corrosive action on metals, and, if not removed after brazing operations, it will cause corrosion and the accumulation of a green substance called "verdigris." This verdigris is a poison, and its accumulation should be discouraged by careful washing off of all particles of flux remaining after brazing.

**Method of Heating.**—When heavy and thin metals are to be joined together, care should be taken so that the thinner metal is not overheated. An example is the brazing of a thin copper pipe to a heavy-cast silver-solder coupling. If the same amount of heat were applied to the pipe as to the casting, the pipe would be overheated and probably burned. In soft soldering, the same care must be exercised when applying heat, or the solder on the thinner metal will be likely to burn before the heavier metal is warm enough to melt the solder.

It is very seldom that two metals of equal thickness are brazed together. In most cases one metal is much heavier than the other, and, when brazed, the heavy metal needs more heat applied to it in order to bring both parts to the brazing heat together. This problem is ever-present in brazing of all kinds, and so practice and experience are necessary. The problems are seldom identical, and the coppersmith must depend on his own judgment for the method of applying the heat.

Since the main object in brazing is to bring both parts to be joined to the brazing heat together, the metals must be heated with discrimination. When first applying heat, bring the white flame of the acetylene torch very close to the work. Keep the torch moving in a circle until the whole circumference of the pipe is preheated (or dark red in color). Then take great care that the torch does not sear or burn through the metal. Keep the inner white point away from red-hot metals because once the metal is red-hot, it is very easily burned (melted) if touched by the white point of heat. To prove this, the coppersmith should experiment with a piece of scrap metal. Apply the heat by laying the white point directly on the metal, holding it there until the metal melts or sears. At another section of the same piece, apply the heat with a circular motion as recommended. This simple experiment will show what to avoid in heating, and the best application of heat to prevent burning the metals.

The following general recommendations for silver brazing are taken from Navy Specifications, Appendix VII, Welding, Part C, Section C-11.

### THE SILVER BRAZING OF FERROUS AND NONFERROUS METALS

**A. Recommended Technique for Preparing the Joints.**—1. The pipe or tube ends shall be cut off square and all burrs shall be removed. When preparing tube ends as required, it is recommended that a coarse hack saw (16 tooth), pipe-cutting machine, or lathe be used. When using a hack saw, it should be suitably guided in a tube cutting-off vise. Care should be taken not to upset or flatten the tube during this operation.

2. All pipe or tube ends shall be sized before assembly to conform to the "Permissible Variations in Clearances between the Fitting and Tube," as tabulated in Fig. 6.

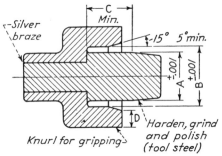

FIG. 6.—Sizing tool for reforming tube ends to proper size and tolerance.

| Fitting size, in. | A, in. | B, in. | C, in. | D, in. |
|---|---|---|---|---|
| $\frac{1}{4}$ | 0.400 | 0.540 | $3\frac{3}{64}$ | $\frac{1}{4}$ |
| $\frac{3}{8}$ | 0.535 | 0.675 | $\frac{9}{16}$ | $\frac{1}{4}$ |
| $\frac{1}{2}$ | 0.700 | 0.840 | $\frac{5}{8}$ | $\frac{1}{4}$ |
| $\frac{3}{4}$ | 0.910 | 1.050 | $2\frac{13}{32}$ | $\frac{1}{4}$ |
| 1 | 1.175 | 1.315 | $1\frac{11}{16}$ | $\frac{3}{8}$ |
| $1\frac{1}{4}$ | 1.520 | 1.660 | $\frac{3}{4}$ | $\frac{3}{8}$ |
| $1\frac{1}{2}$ | 1.760 | 1.900 | $\frac{7}{8}$ | $\frac{7}{16}$ |
| 2 | 2.235 | 2.375 | $2\frac{7}{32}$ | $\frac{1}{2}$ |

PERMISSIBLE VARIATIONS IN CLEARANCES BETWEEN FITTING AND TUBE

| Size, In. | Standard Clearance, In. |
|---|---|
| $\frac{1}{4}$–$\frac{1}{2}$ inclusive | 0.000–0.005 |
| $\frac{3}{4}$–1 inclusive | 0.000–0.006 |
| $1\frac{1}{4}$ | 0.000–0.007 |
| $1\frac{1}{2}$–2 inclusive | 0.000–0.009 |

A proper fit between the tubing and the fitting or flange which makes up the joint is essential to ensure a proper flow of the silver-brazing alloy (silver solder). The permissible variation of the outside diameter of the pipe or tube and of the socket bore of the fitting or flange, as required by Navy Department specifications, provides for this proper fit at the time the material is manufactured. Because of handling and shop operations, the fit of the tubing may be altered. Before proceeding further, all tube ends should be sized as required.

When sizing a pipe or tube of 2-in. pipe size or smaller, a sizing tool similar to the one shown in Fig. 6 may be used. Tube rolls may also be used. Heating of the pipe or tube ends prior to sizing is recommended, and care should be taken not to heat the pipe or tube more than is required for the brazing operation.

Sizing pipe and tube 2½-in. pipe size and larger may be accomplished by bumping or tapping out the high and low spots. The use of a hardwood or light metal ring to check the circularity is recommended. The proper fit should be determined by slipping the fitting or flange onto the pipe or tube end and twisting or turning the fitting or flange. Any remaining high spots should be dressed down, removing as little metal from the pipe or tube as possible.

3. After the pipe or tube has been sized, a light scribe line or other equivalent marking shall be made on the pipe or tube at a distance of 1 in. plus the depth of the socket from the end as shown in Fig. 7.

Scribing of pipe or tube as required above need not be done on flanges unless assembly in the ship or shop prevents observation of the interior of the assembled joints.

4. The inside of the socket and the outside of the pipe or tube for a length greater than the depth of the socket shall be cleaned to bright metal, removing all foreign substances such as oil, scale, and oxides. The cleaned surfaces shall not be handled.

For cleaning surfaces to be brazed, the use of sandpaper or emery cloth of medium fineness is recommended.

5. Silver brazing flux shall be applied evenly to each joint surface immediately after cleaning. If the flux dries before the joint is assembled, a fresh coat of brazing flux shall be applied.

It is recommended that a small brush be used in applying silver brazing flux to cleaned surfaces.

6. The pipe or tube end, or the male end, of a reducing or street-type fitting, shall be inserted to the full depth of the socket. The scribed line, as required, shall be not more than 1 in. beyond the fitting.

7. Prior to brazing, the piping shall be adequately supported and so arranged that expansion and contraction will not be restricted, in order that no strains will be placed on the joints during the brazing and cooling periods.

8. Joints which have been assembled but not brazed within 24 hr. shall be disassembled and refluxed.

**B. Recommended Technique for Heating the Joints.** 1. *Type of Heat.*—Heating of the joint shall be performed with an oxyacetylene welding torch or other torch equipment giving equivalent results, unless other means of heating are approved by the Bureau.

Care should be taken to select the proper size of torch tips for the work to be performed. [Table VI gives author's recommendation for size of tips for various piping sizes.] Medium-pressure torches, designated to give a low velocity, or soft-burning, flame are recommended for this work.

The use of goggles when operating the heating torch is recommended: Goggles having glass not lighter than shade 2 may be used.

2. *Heat Regulation.*—Only sufficient heat shall be applied to the work to cause the brazing alloy to flow.

A slightly reducing flame should be applied to the entire circumference of the pipe or tube in such a manner that the cone of the flame is not nearer than ½ to 1 in. to the end of the fitting or flange in order to expand the pipe or tube. When the flux at the end of the fitting or flange becomes fluid, the pipe or tube has expanded sufficiently. The

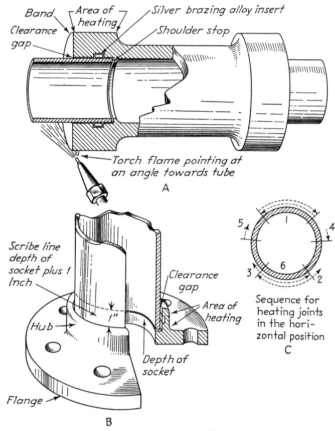

Fig. 7.—Silver brazing.

flame should then be applied to the fitting or flange at the heating area shown in *A* and *B*, Fig. 7. The flame should be pointed in the direction of the pipe or tube in order to keep the pipe or tube at the proper temperature while heating the fitting or flange. The heating torch should be given a rotary or wiping motion over the length of the joint for a width of 1½ to 2 in., until the flux at the end of the fitting or flange becomes very fluid.

3. *The End-feed Type of Fitting.*—After the flux becomes very fluid, heating should continue for 5 or 6 sec., after which the silver brazing alloy should be laid firmly against the heated pipe or tube at the junction with the fitting or flange. Direct contact of the torch flame with the silver brazing alloy should be avoided, particularly with Grade III alloy. Only the heat of the work should melt the brazing alloy. If the heat of the work is not sufficient to cause the brazing alloy to flow into the clearance space, the heating procedure should be repeated. If a red color shows on either the pipe, tube, fitting, or flange, heating should be discontinued at that particular spot until the temperature has dropped. Puddling, or the formation of small pools of molten alloy, should be avoided. When one segment of the joint is completed, the flame should be applied to an adjacent segment, except that for joints brazed in horizontal fixed lines, the heating sequence outlined in *C*, Fig. 7, should be used, until the clearance space is filled as above. This procedure should be followed until the complete circumference of the joint is filled. A satisfactory joint shows a continuous ring of brazing alloy at the end of the fitting or flange socket. When heavy sections of piping, fittings, and flanges, specifically, standard flanges $2\frac{1}{2}$ in. and larger after the entire circumference has been filled, are being brazed, the heating flame should be applied to the entire circumference of the pipe or tube adjacent to the fitting or flange in order to prevent too rapid cooling of the pipe or tube and resultant cracking of the silver brazing alloy. The above post heating should be done with a rotary or wiping motion and should continue for approximately $\frac{1}{2}$ min. per inch of pipe or tube diameter, *i.e.*, for a 4-in. diameter pipe or tube, 2 min. Care should be exercised not to overheat piping, fitting, or flange during this operation.

4. *Fittings with Pre-inserted Silver Solder Band.*—After the flux becomes very fluid, heating should continue for 5 or 6 sec., after which the flame should be removed from this area, so as to allow the fitting or flange to contract and thus force the melted brazing alloy into the clearance space. This should complete the segment of the joint. If a red color shows on either pipe, tube, fitting, or flange, heating should be discontinued at that particular spot until the temperature has dropped. If sufficient brazing alloy does not flow out to fill the clearance space following the above operation, this portion of the joint should be reheated as before, to allow further expansion and contraction of the fittings or flange, in order to force out more brazing alloy. When one segment of the joint is completed, the flame should be applied to an adjacent segment, except that on joints brazed in horizontal fixed lines the heating sequence outlined in *C*, Fig. 7, should be used until the clearance space is filled as above. This procedure should be followed until the complete circumference of the joint is filled. A satisfactory

joint shows a continuous ring of brazing alloy at the end of the fitting or flange socket. When brazing heavy sections of piping, fittings, and flanges, specifically, standard flanges 2½ in. and larger, after the entire circumference has been filled, the heating flame should be applied to the entire circumference of the pipe or tube adjacent to the fitting or flange in order to prevent too rapid cooling of the pipe or tube, and resultant cracking of the silver brazing alloy. The above post heating should be done with a rotary or wiping motion and should continue for approximately ½ min. per inch of pipe or tube diameter, i.e., for a 4-in.-diameter pipe or tube, 2 min. Care should be exercised not to overheat piping, fitting, or flange during this operation.

5. *Cleaning the Joint after Brazing.*—After the brazing operation has been completed, the assembled joint shall be shielded from drafts and cooled slowly. After the work has become hand cool, it shall be thoroughly wire brushed and washed, preferably with hot water, to remove all excess scale, flux, and discolorations.

6. *Tests and Inspection.*—Exterior examination of the joints shall show a complete ring of silver brazing alloy between the pipe or tube and the outer end of the fitting. Surfaces of the joint shall be free of globules of silver brazing alloy. Fillets shall be avoided; however, if formed, they shall be concave and of the minimum practicable dimension.

**C. Detailed Recommendations.**—1. For shop fabrication of flanges the best results are obtained when the joint is brazed in the vertical position, i.e., with the face of the flange down and the pipe or tube extending vertically upward from the flange hub (B, Fig. 7). In this position, the brazing alloy is free to flow with the added aid of gravity to the full depth of the socket.

2. All parts of unions and union ends of fittings, other than valves, should be screwed together hand tight before being heated. Such procedure tends to prevent local overheating and oxidation of the union-joint ground surfaces. Where only half the union is available at the assembly, spare unions or shop unions, either iron or brass, should be provided.

3. Union-end and brazed-end valves should be open (i.e., stems raised) while being heated. This position of the stem tends to prevent burning of the valve packing. Where practicable, the valve body should not be on the union during the heating of the latter, which may be protected by the use of spare union parts.

4. While the heating and brazing operations do not discolor the valve bonnet, nevertheless, to protect the valve packing, the bonnet should be wrapped with a wet swab.

5. To disassemble or take apart joints, the fitting or the tube must be firmly anchored or held before starting the heating in order that the

two parts can be separated or pulled apart at the proper moment. The torch flame should be directed on the entire circumference of the fitting

TABLE III.—SILVER-BRAZING ALLOYS
(Navy Department Specification 47-S-13)

| Material | Method | Grade |
|---|---|---|
| 70-30 to 70-30 | Insert | IV |
| 70-30 to 70-30 | Face feed | III |
| 70-30 to 70-30 | Face feed | IV |
| 70-30 to bronze | Insert | III |
| 70-30 to bronze | Face feed | III |
| 70-30 to bronze | Face feed | IV |
| Copper to bronze | Insert | III |
| Copper to bronze | Face feed | III |
| Copper to copper | Insert | III |
| Copper to copper | Face feed | III |
| C.R.S. to C.R.S. | Insert | IV |
| C.R.S. to C.R.S. | Face feed | IV |
| C.R.S. to steel | Insert | IV |
| C.R.S. to steel | Face feed | IV |
| Steel to steel | Insert | IV |
| Steel to steel | Face feed | IV |
| 70-30 to steel | Insert | IV |
| 70-30 to steel | Face feed | IV |
| Copper to steel | Insert | IV |
| Copper to steel | Face feed | IV |

TABLE IV.—SILVER-BRAZING ALLOYS, CHEMICAL COMPOSITION
(Navy Department Spec. 47-S-13)

| Grade | Silver, per cent | Copper, per cent | Zinc, per cent | Phosphorus, per cent | Cadmium, per cent | Nickel, per cent | Impurities, per cent |
|---|---|---|---|---|---|---|---|
| 0 | 19–21 | 44–46 | 33–37 | | | | 0.15 |
| I | 44–46 | 29–31 | 23–27 | | | | .15 |
| II | 64–66 | 19–21 | 13–17 | | | | .15 |
| III | 14.5–15.5 | 79–81 | | 4.75–5.25 | | | .15 |
| IV | 49–51 | 14.5–16.5 | 14.5–18.5 | | 17–19 | | .15 |
| V | 49–51 | 14.5–16.5 | 13.5–17.5 | | 15–17 | 2.5–3.5 | .15 |

bead to expand it away from the tube. The same wiping or rotary movement mentioned in paragraph 3, page 39, should be used. As soon as the bead becomes expanded and shows a dull-red color, the brazing alloy will be softened enough so that the fitting can be slipped off. A slight rocking motion of the fitting or tube aids considerably in slipping it off the tube when hot. The fittings, flanges, and valves should not be hammered while hot when being disassembled or when being removed from a line.

1. Grade III brazing alloy is furnished in the following sizes:

Strips 0.050 by $\frac{1}{16}$ by 20 in.

Strips 0.050 by $\frac{1}{8}$ by 20 in.

Rod $\frac{1}{8}$ in. square by 36 in.

2. Grades IV and V are furnished in the following sizes of wire:

$\frac{1}{32}$, $\frac{1}{16}$, $\frac{3}{32}$, and $\frac{1}{8}$ in. in diameter.

3. Uses:

*a.* Silver brazing alloys are intended for joints requiring higher physical properties than provided by soft or spelter solders. Silver brazing alloys are used ordinarily at operating temperatures not exceeding 425°F., for strength joints, and at temperatures up to 200°F. below the melting point, for sealing mechanical joints.

*b.* Except as noted in paragraphs *c, d* and *e,* the selection of the particular grade should be based on the expected service temperature and color of the completed joint.

*c.* Grade III silver brazing alloy is intended for brazing only copper and copper-base alloys. It should never be used on ferrous alloys.

*d.* Grade IV silver brazing alloy is intended for joining nickel-copper alloys and plain carbon and alloy steels.

*e.* Grade V silver brazing alloy is intended for those applications where the characteristics of Grade IV are required but where the design of the job necessitates the addition of a fillet or where close tolerances cannot be maintained and the filling is necessary. Grade V is intended also for hard materials such as cemented carbides for tools.

*f.* Thin, narrow strips of grade I, II, IV, and V silver brazing alloy should be used for very light work, such as joining parts of delicate instruments.

4. The approximate melting points, flow points, and colors of the grades of silver brazing alloys are as follows:

TABLE V

| Grade | Melting point, °F. | Flow point, °F. | Color |
|:---:|:---:|:---:|:---|
| 0 | 1430 | 1500 | Yellow |
| I | 1250 | 1370 | Nearly white |
| II | 1280 | 1325 | White |
| III | 1200 | 1300 | Gray-white |
| IV | 1160 | 1175 | Yellow-white |
| V | 1195 | 1270 | Yellow-white |

**Acetylene Torch and Its Uses.**—The use of the acetylene torch by the coppersmith is increasing each year because it is very useful for silver brazing and also because the torch is a means of quick, portable heat. It is especially handy when working aboard ship, making pipe installations, or repairing old work, because the flame is small and very intense, and the heat can be controlled and confined directly to the parts being brazed. It has become more important since the development of the various low-temperature silver solders and the special fluxes, but the use of acetylene is not confined to silver brazing alone, as it is now used generally throughout the trade. The operation of the acetylene torch has, in the past, been confined to specialists, acetylene welders or burners, but now every coppersmith is required to be able to handle acetylene as a part of his trade.

TABLE VI.—SUGGESTED TIP SIZES FOR SILVER BRAZING*

| Pipe size | Tip size No. | Oxygen, lb. pressure | Acetylene, lb. pressure | Pipe size | Tip size No. | Oxygen, lb. pressure | Acetylene, lb. pressure |
|---|---|---|---|---|---|---|---|
| ¼ | 4 | 8 | 6 | 2½ | 6 | 12 | 10 |
| ⅜ | 4 | 8 | 6 | 3 | 8 | 12 | 10 |
| ½ | 6 | 12 | 10 | 4 | 8 | 15 | 12 |
| ¾ | 6 | 12 | 10 | 4½ | 8 | 15 | 12 |
| 1 | 6 | 12 | 10 | 5 | 8 | 15 | 12 |
| 1¼ | 6 | 12 | 10 | 6 | 9 | 20 | 15 |
| 1½ | 6 | 12 | 10 | 8 | 9 | 20 | 15 |
| 2 | 6 | 12 | 10 | 10 | 10 | 20 | 15 |

* This chart is merely a guide, or starting point, based on general practice; it should not be adhered to strictly.

The setting of the gauges of the acetylene torch depends largely on the type of torch used.

The ideal clearance for fits on silver-brazing jobs is from 2 to 3 thousandths. On the large fittings the clearances are as much as 10 thousandths to facilitate fitting. This excess clearance is taken care of by peening the copper snugly against the flange or fitting.

Make good fits. Never use silver solder as a filler. To a limited extent it is easier to regulate the torch flame at the blow-pipe valve than to change tips for each size of pipe.

**Types of Acetylene-flame Adjustment.**—There are four general types of flame adjustment on an oxyacetylene torch: (1) the acetylene flame, no oxygen; (2) carburizing or reducing flame, slightly excess acetylene; (3) neutral flame, balanced oxygen and acetylene; and (4) oxidizing flame, excess oxygen (see Fig. 8).

1. The acetylene flame produces a blinding white heat. It is produced by opening the acetylene valve only. This flame is impractical for any heating use.

2. The carburizing, reducing, or three-cone flame, is slightly excess acetylene. In this flame there are three definite colors, a white flame at the torch tip changing slightly to a greenish-white cone and then again to a wide blue about 3 to 4 in. long. The bluish-white cone is placed directly on the metal to be brazed and is kept moving constantly. The inner white cone should not touch the work. This flame is best for all-round annealing and brazing operations.

3. Neutral flame is obtained by a proper balance of acetylene and oxygen. The white acetylene tip on this flame is reduced to a small rounded point about $\frac{3}{8}$ in. long, more or less, depending on the size of the tip used. The neutral flame is commonly used and is fair for coppersmithing operations but must be handled with great care because the white tip on this flame is extremely hot (about 6300°F.) and should not come in contact with the work while the work is red-hot, during annealing or brazing.

4. Oxidizing flame is excess oxygen flame. This flame is nearly all blue in color, and the white tip is reduced to a very small blunt point. This flame is not to be used in coppersmithing operations. It is the type of flame used in acetylene torches for cutting through steel.

**Brazing with an Acetylene Torch.**—Low- or high-temperature brazing of both large and small work can be done with the acetylene torch. Large or heavy work should be preheated with large kerosene or gas torches or with a forge. After being preheated to a red, or annealing, color, the acetylene torch is used at the points of the braze. Great care should be exercised by the workman applying heat with an acetylene torch when metal is red-hot, because if the white tip touches the metal being brazed, the acetylene will melt it. When copper or brass is being brazed, the heat should be adjusted to a reducing, or three-cone flame (see Fig. 8).

Acetylene Flame
(no oxygen)

Reducing Flame
(slightly excess acetylene)

Neutral Flame
(Balanced oxygen and acetylene)

Oxidizing Flame
(excess oxygen)

FIG. 8.—Acetylene flames.

**Other Uses of an Acetylene Torch.**—Small pipe-bending and annealing operations are also done with acetylene heat. Soldering and sweating operations of a small size may be done, although the torch must be used with care and good judgment to prevent overheating and burning the tin. The blue section of the neutral flame is recommended for soldering and tinning small work.

Other uses of acetylene heat are for reducing a pipe; for keeping work hot while it is being hammered, so that there is no delay for annealing; for heating saddle branches while they are being roughed out (thus completing the job in one continuous operation); for applying heat locally when flanging copper on Van Stone operations; and for hot-working copper in general. The advantage is that the workman can hold the torch in one hand, heating the work, while hammering with the other hand.

**Localized Heating.**—The ability to control heat by confining it to the immediate area of the operation is a valuable aid in shipwork when the work is surrounded by electric cables or other inflammable matter. By wrapping electric cables with asbestos cloth or protecting them from the acetylene flame with an asbestos sheet, the coppersmith can silver braze safely within a few inches of the cables. Such local control of heat makes the acetylene torch and silver brazing valuable in modern shipbuilding.

Controlled heat is also valuable in fitting pipe aboard ship, in tacking operations, in annealing, in heating sections of pipe to relieve strain, in patching work in general, and making emergency repairs of various kinds.

**Safety Factors in Silver Brazing.**—Wear goggles when brazing. Be especially careful when the work is overhead because molten solder or flux may drop.

Protect the eyes from the blinding flame by wearing goggles while working with an acetylene torch.

Whenever possible, avoid working directly over the braze, as the fumes from silver flux are poisonous and harmful. Avoid getting any flux on open cuts or on the hands when fluxing work, as a skin rash may develop. Apply flux with a brush and not with your fingers.

Be extremely careful when handling a lighted torch that it does not touch yourself or a fellow workman. Serious burns may be inflicted by merely touching the flesh.

The safety precautions should be strictly observed in connection with the handling and care of the oxyacetylene torch, hose, gauges, and flasks.

Read the following instructions taken from the Deep-Sea Diving School Manual on Operating Rules for the Gas Torch.

### GAS TORCH

#### GENERAL OPERATING RULES

*Read, remember, and observe these rules.*
*Many of them are law in some localities.*

1. Caution! Important! Use No Oil! Never allow oil or grease to come in contact with oxygen. It is dangerous, and lubrication of apparatus is not necessary.

2. Do not allow the hose to come in contact with oil or grease because it will penetrate the rubber.

3. Before connecting the blowpipe, blow out both hoses.

4. Every week disconnect the blowpipe and blow out both hoses. It is important that the inside of the hose be kept clean so that dirt or small particles of rubber will not be carried into the blowpipe passageways and clog them.

5. Always use the green hose for oxygen and the red hose for acetylene. Do not interchange the hoses.

6. Always see that the hoses are securely clamped to the blowpipe and regulators before using.

7. Always protect the hose from being run over or trampled on; avoid tangles and kinks.

8. Examine the hoses occasionally for leaks by putting pressure in them and immersing them in water.

9. Always use the proper tip or nozzle and the proper pressure for the work at hand as shown on the pressure chart.

10. In case the flame backfires, immediately close the blowpipe oxygen needle valve for a moment and then reopen. Relight it if necessary.

11. When a new cylinder is connected to the apparatus, always open the blowpipe valves a sufficient time to expel any air from the hose before lighting.

12. When a new cylinder is connected to the apparatus, do not light the blowpipe until you are positive the regulator is adjusted to the proper working pressure.

13. Do not hang a blowpipe and its hose on either the regulators or the cylinder valves.

14. Never clean out a blowpipe tip or nozzle with a sharp, hard tool. Use a soft copper or brass wire.

15. For packing valves use Oxweld Treated Packing. If this is not available, use asbestos cord packing impregnated with glycerine.

16. Always wear goggles when working with the lighted blowpipe.

17. When working in a confined place, always have a helper near by to close the cylinder valves in case of necessity.

18. Before starting work see that there is sufficient oxygen and acetylene on hand to complete the job.

19. Before connecting a regulator to a cylinder, open the cylinder valve just enough to blow out any dirt present so that it will not be carried into the regulator and cause leakage or creeping. Close the valve quickly to avoid wasting gas.

20. Before opening a cylinder valve (the regulator having been attached) release the pressure-adjusting handle on the regulator by turning it to the left.

21. Never tighten a leaky regulator to cylinder connection without first closing the cylinder valve.

22. Do not decrease the pressure or release the pressure-adjusting handle by turning it to the left while the low-pressure gauge indicates pressure, unless the blowpipe valve is open.

23. Do not leave pressure in the regulators when not in use. The pressure gauges will indicate this.

24. Before disconnecting a regulator from a cylinder, release the pressure-adjusting handle by turning it to the left.

25. Always insert the dust plug in the regulator union nut when the regulator is not attached to a cylinder.

26. Always first barely crack cylinder valves to let the high-pressure gauge hand move up slowly. Then open them the rest of the way. Do not crack valves enough to cause the gauge hand to move quickly.

27. Always open oxygen-cylinder valves fully.

28. Never open acetylene-cylinder valves more than $1\frac{1}{2}$ full turns.

29. Always close cylinder valves when the work is finished.

30. Always close cylinder valves tightly even though the cylinders are considered empty.

31. Always use the wrench provided for the acetylene-cylinder valve.

32. Always leave the wrench on acetylene-cylinder valve when in use.

33. Always stand acetylene cylinders on end. Never lay them down.

34. Do not use the top of the acetylene cylinder as a receptacle for tools.

35. Never tamper with cylinder fuse plugs.

36. Never tamper with or attempt to repair oxygen-cylinder valves.

37. Do not handle cylinders roughly.

38. When transporting cylinders by means of a crane, use a cradle. Do not use slings.

39. Never use an electric magnet for handling cylinders.

## CARE OF APPARATUS,
### LIGHTING THE TORCH, AND SHUTTING IT OFF

1. Do not use oil or grease on cylinder valves, regulators, or torches·
2. Do not light torch with both torch valves open.
3. Do not use leaking or damaged apparatus. If a cylinder valve leaks, take the cylinder out of the shop and notify the shipper at once. If torches or regulators leak, have them repaired and tested by the manufacturer. If hose leaks, *immediately exchange it for good hose.*
4. Keep hose from kinking, free from obstructions, and do not use excessive hose lengths.
5. Keep the torch flame and sparks away from hose, regulators, and cylinders. Keep hose away from heated metal.
6. Close cylinder valves when not in actual use.
7. Do not tighten the regulator-adjusting screw to the limit in order to bleed the cylinders.
8. Regulator-adjusting screws should be released when not in use.

### STARTING

1. Open cylinder valves slowly, to blow out any dirt before connecting regulators to valves, and then close valves.
2. Connect regulators to cylinder valves, with regulator-adjusting screw released; make sure that connecting seats are clean, free from grease or bruises, before connecting. Set the connecting nuts up tightly with the proper wrench and carefully avoid crossing threads.
3. Open acetylene-cylinder valve one full turn; open the oxygen-cylinder valve slowly, fully open.
4. Connect hose to regulators and blow out hose with gas to free it from dust or dirt before connecting to torch, by turning in regulator-adjusting screw, then releasing screw to close regulator.
5. Connect torch to hose. Standard oxygen connections have right-hand threads; acetylene connections, left-hand threads. Set nuts up tightly with proper wrench, making sure that connecting seats are clean and free from bruises to avoid leaks.
6. Use only tips that have clean seats, free from bruises. A bruised or dented tip makes a leaky seat and scores the torch head, making repairs necessary. Using a larger size tip than necessary wastes gas and is likely to result in poor work.
7. Open torch acetylene needle valve, with the oxygen valve closed; turn in acetylene regulator-adjusting screw until the low-pressure gauge registers the desired working pressure; close acetylene needle valve. Then adjust oxygen regulator for the required working pressure; close oxygen needle valve.

8. Open acetylene needle valve and light torch with spark lighter; open oxygen needle valve and adjust for neutral welding flame.

9. Set the working pressures at the regulators slightly higher than required tip pressures, and adjust the flame with torch needle valves; this is done to avoid frequent readjustment of the regulators to compensate for falling pressures.

### STOPPING

1. Close acetylene valve on torch first.
2. Close oxygen valve on torch.
3. Close acetylene-cylinder valve.
4. Close oxygen-cylinder valve.
5. Open torch acetylene valve, with oxygen valve closed, to drain the line; release the adjusting screw on the acetylene regulator and then promptly close torch acetylene valve.
6. Open torch oxygen valve, with acetylene valve closed, to drain the line; release the adjusting screw of the oxygen regulator, then promptly close torch oxygen valve.
7. Flashbacks result from mixed gases in either oxygen or acetylene hose. By following these rules, acetylene will not get over into the oxygen line nor oxygen into the acetylene line when starting or shutting down. If torch flame is properly adjusted and maintained, with correct pressures, and tip outlets kept free from obstruction in operation, flashbacks will be eliminated.
8. Remove regulators from cylinders when moving cylinders. Replace caps over cylinder valves when cylinders are empty and mark cylinders "MT."

# CHAPTER VII

## FLANGES

Flanges are used as portable connections for joining sections of pipe. A gasket is used as a filler between the flanges to prevent leakage when flanges are bolted together. There are many types and shapes of flanges used in shipbuilding, but the few flanges mentioned here are those most commonly used.

Flanges for coppersmithing can be roughly classified as silver brazing, low and high pressure; spelter brazing, low and high pressure; bulkhead flange (silver and spelter brazing), low and high pressure; and the Van Stone flange. Oval, square, and odd-shaped flanges are sometimes necessary for special jobs; also the various raised face, male and female, ring, and split flanges have their special uses. The shapes and forms of these are too numerous to illustrate.

**Silver-brazing Flanges.**—Silver-brazing flanges are usually made of composition $M$. They are brazed to the pipe with silver solder. The high collar of the flange is especially designed for silver brazing.

**Spelter-brazing Flanges.**—Spelter-brazing flanges are made of composition $F$, with melting point designed for brazing with spelter. This composition is called "brazing metal."

**Bulkhead Flanges.**—Bulkhead flanges, see Fig. 9, may be either composition $M$ or $F$, depending on whether they are to be silver or spelter brazed. The bulkhead flange is used when a portable connection is desired in a line going through a bulkhead. The bulkhead flange has two bolt circles, one for bolting to the bulkhead and one for bolting to the section of pipe on the opposite side of the bulkhead. Special insulators are used on bulkhead flanges when steam lines are run through the bulkheads, insulating the hot pipe from the bulkhead and thus aiding the efficiency of the steam line by preventing the conduction of heat to the bulkhead.

**Standardization of Flanges.**—Since flanges and pipes are standardized, only the I.P.S. (iron-pipe size) has to be known before ordering a flange. The flange standard charts should be consulted when in doubt as to which standard is used, because both the American and Navy standards are used on modern ships.

**Soft Flanges.**—On repair work it is sometimes necessary to use flanges that have a low melting point. These are best brazed

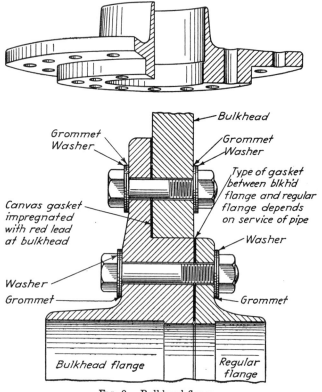

Fig. 9.—Bulkhead flange.

with silver solder. Ordinary spelter can be mixed with Grades III, IV, or V silver solder, about a 50-50 mixture, to make a low-temperature-melting spelter. Borax is used as a flux.

A low-temperature-melting-point flange is yellow when scraped or filed. Yellow brass has a low copper content with a comparatively low melting point. A high-temperature-melting brass has a more reddish color. The red color shows that it has a higher content of copper.

**Salvaging or Reclaiming Old Flanges.**—Flanges from old pipes are easily salvaged and may be used over again on new piping.

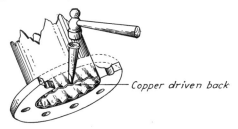

Copper driven back

Holes are filled with mud for safety precaution.
When the entire pipe must be saved, the method
of heating is similar to that of brazing *(see Fig.13)*
Heat the flange until spelter melts; then press
down on flange lightly.
When flange comes off, cut off heat quickly
and remove from pipe

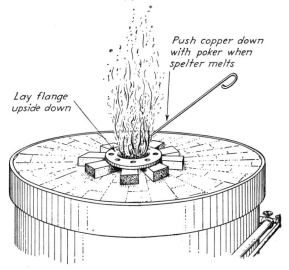

Push copper down
with poker when
spelter melts

Lay flange
upside down

When the entire pipe does not have to be saved,
the pipe is cut next to the flange and laid on the
forge in this manner

Fig. 10.—Reclaiming old flanges.

The reclaimed flanges are in most cases just as good as new, and whenever old work is being renewed the flanges should be salvaged and reused.

Figure 10 shows spelter-brazing flanges being salvaged.   Silver-brazing flanges, as well as many different kinds of fittings, may also be salvaged.   In salvaging spelter-brazing flanges, the method is to crimp the copper inward at the face of the flange (Fig. 10), loosening it as much as possible before placing it on the fire.   When the heat is applied, only the spelter need be melted and then the flange will slip off.   **Do not hammer on the flange while it is red-hot.**

When the flange is loosened from the copper pipe, let it cool until it is black in color before you quench it with acid or water. Grind or file away all the spelter; remove warp from the flange by hammering it with a rawhide mallet while the face of the flange is lying flat on a smooth steel plate or slab.

**Salvaging a Silver-brazed Flange.**—Removing a silver-brazed flange from a pipe is easier than removing the spelter-brazed flange, because the silver-brazed flange is not usually peened to the pipe.   The best method of removing a silver-brazed flange is to hang the pipe over a forge so that the flange is in a downward position about 2 in. above the forge opening.   Place firebricks around the flange and then heat it.   Before starting the forge, plug the opposite openings of the pipe to prevent the flame from shooting through.   When the flange is hot enough to melt the silver, it will come off with a slight push.   **Do not hammer.**

If a forge is not available, the flange may be removed with torches.   While the flange is still red-hot, it should be brushed with a wire brush to remove particles of silver solder.

**Van Stone Flanges.**—Van Stone flanges are in common use in marine and industrial work.   They have one advantage over other flanges in that they are not brazed or soldered but are left loose on the pipe, the copper being turned over against the face of the flange.   Brazing equipment, then, is not necessary when Van Stone flanges are fitted and worked.   Van Stone flanging may be done on the job without sending the pipe to the shop, as is necessary for spelter brazing.

Figure 11 shows the typical procedure for flanging a Van Stone joint.   The copper is turned over at the face of the flange to form the seat for a joint.   A gasket is used on the face of the copper, just as on ordinary flanges, when installing.   The Van Stone flange is a thicker and larger flange than the ordinary brazing flanges.   The thickness is necessary to keep it from warping while being bolted up. Steel flanges are best and are used almost entirely for this purpose.

The weak point in the Van Stone joint (see Fig. 11) is its tendency to crystallize and break from vibration and working stress. These breaks occur at the turned-over radius of the copper. While Van Stone joints are used on copper lines, they

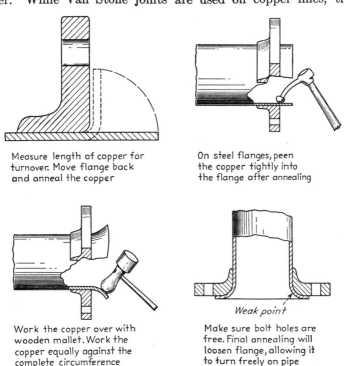

Measure length of copper for turnover. Move flange back and anneal the copper

On steel flanges, peen the copper tightly into the flange after annealing

Work the copper over with wooden mallet. Work the copper equally against the complete circumference of the face

Make sure bolt holes are free. Final annealing will loosen flange, allowing it to turn freely on pipe

*Weak point*

Fig. 11.—Van Stone flanging.

should be used only as emergency joints because the brazed or silver-brazed flange is far superior from the standpoint of service without leaks over a period of years.

**Large Van Stone Flanges.**—It is comparatively easy to place large Van Stone flanges on pipes that are fitted in a shop template, and this ease tends to make the Van Stone flange popular when speed of manufacture is most essential.

In the operations of fitting a Van Stone flanged pipe from 8 in. I.P.S. diameter on up, where exact face-to-face measurements are necessary, a wooden template is built aboard ship (see Fig. 34), and a target is built in the shop.  The pipe is made to fit a center wire, and then the flanges are slipped on.  The pipe with the loosely set flanges is slipped into the shop template.  The plates of the shop target should have the centers cut out to allow the pipe to slip through.  A sliding target is necessary on most large work.

The sliding target is made by constructing one of the target ends so that it is movable in a track built of two side planks and smooth bottom plates, with a stopper at the face of the target plate.  This sliding target, when opened, will allow the long pipe to be slipped through the hole.  Then the plate is pushed tightly against the stopper, and the sliding target is screwed or tacked solidly into place.  The gaskets that are needed for fitting the pipe should be tacked on the face of the target, and, in addition to the gasket, another gasket of the thickness of the side wall of the pipe should be tacked to allow for the Van Stone turnover of the copper.  When these two thicknesses of gasket are in place, pull the flanges up to the plates and bolt them on.  While the pipe is solidly secured in place, the copper should be peened against the inside of the flange as shown in Van Stone (Fig. 11).  The pipe should then be removed and trimmed for the proper turnover on the face, and the copper hammered against the flange.  It is good practice to try the pipe in the target again to see how it fits.  But, of course, the extra thickness of gasket that was allowed for turnover should first be removed.  It is also advisable, when the pipe is in the template being peened, to make scribe marks on the back of the flange and on the copper so that the flange may be checked in case it moves during the flanging process.

**Forge Setup.**—Figure 13 shows a typical forge setup for spelter brazing a flange.  Although this method of brazing is not done very often since the advent of silver and acetylene brazing, this setup may be used to advantage to preheat large flanges for acetylene brazing or to remove silver- or spelter-brazing flanges.

Before spelter brazing the flange, fill the holes and coat the top of the flange itself with a layer of tinker's clay to prevent the spelter from flowing onto the flange and to prevent melting the flange.  (Figure 12 illustrates fitting, peening, and mudding.)  When ready to braze, adjust the pipe so that the flange hangs

level over the hole of the forge. The top of the flange should be
level with the top of the firebricks. Place the firebricks against
the side of the flange, arranging them so that they fit tightly
against each other and against the flange.

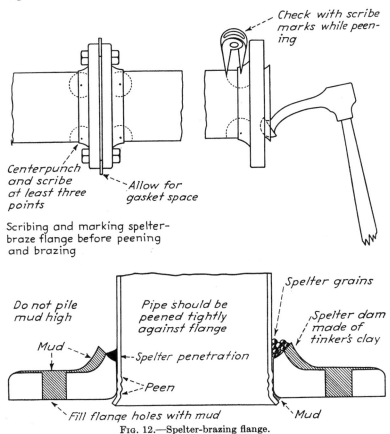

Fig. 12.—Spelter-brazing flange.

Plug the pipe with a metal or wood plug to prevent the fire
from blowing through. The plugging will also prevent overheating of the pipe by allowing the heat to concentrate at the
flange and at the lower part of the pipe. For large-diameter pipe
brazing, the sheet-metal plug is set in the bottom end of the
pipe, about 2 in. above the flange. The plug, being thus close
to the flange, localizes the heat at the point where the braze
is to be made. This method of placing the metal plug at the

bottom is most satisfactory on large work.  To make the plug flameproof, fire clay should be applied to the openings or gaps.

When the pipe is set up, borax water is poured into the brazing trough to flux the flange and pipe; the water will also show whether the flange needs leveling.   If the trough is level, put in the spelter and then start the forge.   Adjust the flame so that it

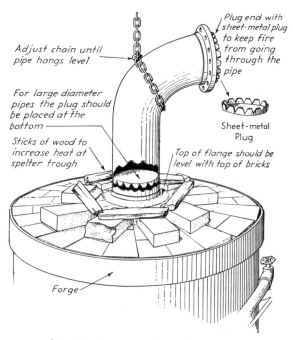

Adjust chain until pipe hangs level

For large diameter pipes the plug should be placed at the bottom

Sticks of wood to increase heat at spelter trough

Plug end with sheet-metal plug to keep fire from going through the pipe

Sheet-metal Plug

Top of flange should be level with top of bricks

Forge

Fig. 13.—Forge setup for spelter brazing.

leaps softly around the flange and onto the pipe.  The wood shown is used to intensify the heat at the top of the flange.  This aids heating the pipe at the brazing trough.

When the brazing point is reached and the spelter is breaking down and melting, extreme care should be taken so that the flange or pipe is not overheated.  Usually one side of the braze melts quicker than the other.  When spelter melts at one side, remove the wood from that side and place it where the spelter has not yet melted.  This helps to heat one side while reducing the heat on the opposite side.  When the spelter is melted completely around and the job is smooth, shut off the heat and remove all wood.

This procedure is used on flanges up to 5 or 6 in. I.P.S. Larger sizes are done in the same manner except that after being preheated they are brazed at the surface with a torch instead of depending on the wood alone. The surface heat may be supplied by either a kerosene, gas, or an acetylene torch, whereas the forge is used mostly for preheating.

Points to remember when brazing a flange:

Make sure that the pipe is peened thoroughly to the flange.

Make sure that the work is cleaned and fluxed.

Do not pile the mud high; this only retards heating.

Hang the flange level.

Plug the pipe.

**Flanges, Silver or Spelter Brazed.**—All flanges, no matter whether they are designed for spelter or silver brazing, can be brazed with silver solder. Flanges can be silver brazed either aboard ship or in the shop, whereas spelter brazing of flanges is strictly a shop operation and requires more skill and also transportation to and from the job before final completion. For this reason, the trend of coppersmithing is toward the use of silver alloys, which are low melting and can be completed on the spot with an acetylene torch.

When small flanges are silver brazed, the complete operation is easily done with an acetylene torch; no mud or forge is necessary. A forge or large torch may be used when a preheat is necessary to prevent warp in a large surface and at the same time to speed the work.

**Riveted and Sweated Flange.**—Riveted flanges are often used on large-diameter pipes. They are riveted and then sweated with solder to make them watertight. The advantages of a riveted and sweated flange are that the work can be done when a high temperature is not available, and it is much simpler from the standpoint of shop equipment.

**Operations in Riveting and Sweating a Flange** (see Fig. 14).—Fit the pipe to the flange and drill the holes through both flange and pipe. When one hole is drilled, place a bolt in it. Next drill a hole directly opposite, placing a bolt in the drilled hole. After three or four holes have been drilled and bolted, the rest of them may be drilled without bolting. Remove the flange from

the pipe.  Tin the flange, pipe, and rivets.  Place the flange
on the pipe; put three or four bolts opposite each other into the
rivet holes to hold the flange in place and then rivet both parts
together.  After riveting, peen the copper over at the face of

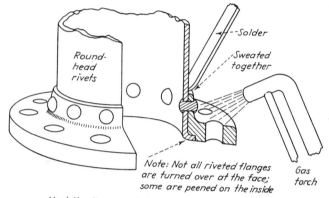

Heat the flange and pipe around the complete
circumference gradually with a soft heat

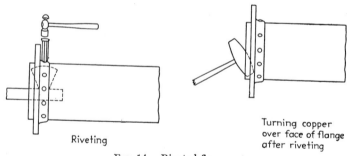

Riveting

Turning copper
over face of flange
after riveting

Fig. 14.—Riveted flange.

the flange.  Swab the rivets, the pipe, and the flange with cut
acid, and then heat with a torch.  Flood the flange collar and
rivets inside and outside and the face of the flange with solder.
After cooling until the solder is firm, the flange and pipe should
be washed clean with cold water.  File away all lumps and dress
down the flange face.

### TABLE VII.—LOW-PRESSURE AMERICAN FLANGES

| Size | No. of holes | Diam. | Size of bolt | Pitch circle |
|---|---|---|---|---|
| $\frac{1}{4}$ | 4 | $2\frac{1}{2}$ | $\frac{3}{8}$ | $1\frac{11}{16}$ |
| $\frac{3}{8}$ | 4 | $2\frac{1}{2}$ | $\frac{3}{8}$ | $1\frac{11}{16}$ |
| $\frac{1}{2}$ | 4 | 3 | $\frac{3}{8}$ | $2\frac{1}{8}$ |
| $\frac{3}{4}$ | 4 | $3\frac{1}{2}$ | $\frac{3}{8}$ | $2\frac{1}{2}$ |
| 1 | 4 | 4 | $\frac{1}{2}$ | 3 |
| $1\frac{1}{4}$ | 4 | $4\frac{1}{2}$ | $\frac{1}{2}$ | $3\frac{3}{8}$ |
| $1\frac{1}{2}$ | 4 | 5 | $\frac{1}{2}$ | $3\frac{7}{8}$ |
| 2 | 4 | 6 | $\frac{5}{8}$ | $4\frac{3}{4}$ |
| $2\frac{1}{2}$ | 4 | 7 | $\frac{5}{8}$ | $5\frac{1}{2}$ |
| 3 | 4 | $7\frac{1}{2}$ | $\frac{5}{8}$ | 6 |
| $3\frac{1}{2}$ | 8 | $8\frac{1}{2}$ | $\frac{5}{8}$ | 7 |
| 4 | 8 | 9 | $\frac{5}{8}$ | $7\frac{1}{2}$ |
| $4\frac{1}{2}$ | 8 | $9\frac{1}{4}$ | $\frac{3}{4}$ | $7\frac{3}{4}$ |
| 5 | 8 | 10 | $\frac{3}{4}$ | $8\frac{1}{2}$ |
| 6 | 8 | 11 | $\frac{3}{4}$ | $9\frac{1}{2}$ |
| 7 | 8 | $12\frac{1}{2}$ | $\frac{3}{4}$ | $10\frac{3}{4}$ |
| 8 | 8 | $13\frac{1}{2}$ | $\frac{3}{4}$ | $11\frac{3}{4}$ |
| 9 | 12 | 15 | $\frac{3}{4}$ | $13\frac{1}{4}$ |

### TABLE VIII.—HIGH-PRESSURE AMERICAN FLANGES

| Size | No. of holes | Size of bolt | Diam. | Pitch circle |
|---|---|---|---|---|
| 1 | 4 | $\frac{1}{2}$ | $4\frac{1}{2}$ | $3\frac{1}{4}$ |
| $1\frac{1}{4}$ | 4 | $\frac{1}{2}$ | 5 | $3\frac{3}{4}$ |
| $1\frac{1}{2}$ | 4 | $\frac{5}{8}$ | 6 | $4\frac{1}{2}$ |
| 2 | 8 | $\frac{5}{8}$ | $6\frac{1}{2}$ | 5 |
| $2\frac{1}{2}$ | 8 | $\frac{3}{4}$ | $7\frac{1}{2}$ | $5\frac{7}{8}$ |
| 3 | 8 | $\frac{3}{4}$ | $8\frac{1}{4}$ | $6\frac{5}{8}$ |
| $3\frac{1}{2}$ | 8 | $\frac{3}{4}$ | 9 | $7\frac{1}{4}$ |
| 4 | 8 | $\frac{3}{4}$ | 10 | $7\frac{7}{8}$ |
| $4\frac{1}{2}$ | 8 | $\frac{3}{4}$ | $10\frac{1}{2}$ | $8\frac{1}{2}$ |
| 5 | 8 | $\frac{3}{4}$ | 11 | $9\frac{1}{4}$ |
| 6 | 12 | $\frac{3}{4}$ | $12\frac{1}{2}$ | $10\frac{5}{8}$ |
| 7 | 12 | $\frac{7}{8}$ | 14 | $11\frac{7}{8}$ |
| 8 | 12 | $\frac{7}{8}$ | 15 | 13 |
| 9 | 12 | 1 | $16\frac{1}{4}$ | 14 |
| 10 | 16 | 1 | $17\frac{1}{2}$ | $15\frac{1}{4}$ |
| 12 | 16 | $1\frac{1}{8}$ | $20\frac{1}{2}$ | $17\frac{3}{4}$ |

TABLE IX.—BUREAU OF ENGINEERING—LOW-PRESSURE BULKHEAD FLANGES,
NAVY STANDARD

| Size | No. of holes | Diam. | Size of bolt | Pitch circle | Pitch chord |
|------|------|------|------|------|------|
| $\frac{1}{4}$ | 6 | $6\frac{1}{16}$ | $\frac{1}{2}$ | $4\frac{7}{8}$ | 2.44 |
| $\frac{1}{2}$ | 6 | $6\frac{3}{16}$ | $\frac{1}{2}$ | $5\frac{1}{16}$ | 2.53 |
| $\frac{3}{4}$ | 8 | $6\frac{7}{16}$ | $\frac{1}{2}$ | $5\frac{5}{16}$ | 2.03 |
| 1 | 8 | $6\frac{7}{8}$ | $\frac{1}{2}$ | $5\frac{3}{4}$ | 2.20 |
| $1\frac{1}{4}$ | 8 | $7\frac{1}{8}$ | $\frac{1}{2}$ | 6 | 2.30 |
| $1\frac{1}{2}$ | 8 | $7\frac{11}{16}$ | $\frac{1}{2}$ | $6\frac{9}{16}$ | 2.51 |
| 2 | 10 | $8\frac{3}{16}$ | $\frac{1}{2}$ | $7\frac{1}{16}$ | 2.18 |
| $2\frac{1}{2}$ | 10 | $8\frac{3}{4}$ | $\frac{1}{2}$ | $7\frac{5}{8}$ | 2.36 |
| 3 | 10 | $9\frac{1}{4}$ | $\frac{1}{2}$ | $8\frac{1}{8}$ | 2.51 |
| $3\frac{1}{2}$ | 10 | $9\frac{13}{16}$ | $\frac{1}{2}$ | $8\frac{11}{16}$ | 2.68 |
| 4 | 12 | $10\frac{5}{16}$ | $\frac{1}{2}$ | $9\frac{3}{16}$ | 2.38 |
| $4\frac{1}{2}$ | 12 | $10\frac{13}{16}$ | $\frac{1}{2}$ | $9\frac{11}{16}$ | 2.51 |
| 5 | 12 | $12\frac{3}{8}$ | $\frac{5}{8}$ | $10\frac{15}{16}$ | 2.83 |
| $5\frac{1}{2}$ | 12 | $12\frac{7}{8}$ | $\frac{5}{8}$ | $11\frac{7}{16}$ | 2.96 |
| 6 | 12 | $13\frac{7}{16}$ | $\frac{5}{8}$ | 12 | 3.11 |
| $6\frac{1}{2}$ | 14 | $13\frac{15}{16}$ | $\frac{5}{8}$ | $12\frac{1}{2}$ | 2.78 |
| 7 | 14 | $14\frac{5}{8}$ | $\frac{5}{8}$ | $13\frac{3}{16}$ | 2.93 |
| $7\frac{1}{2}$ | 14 | $15\frac{3}{16}$ | $\frac{5}{8}$ | $13\frac{3}{4}$ | 3.06 |
| 8 | 14 | $15\frac{11}{16}$ | $\frac{5}{8}$ | $14\frac{1}{4}$ | 3.17 |
| $8\frac{1}{2}$ | 14 | $16\frac{1}{4}$ | $\frac{5}{8}$ | $14\frac{13}{16}$ | 3.29 |
| 9 | 14 | $18\frac{5}{16}$ | $\frac{3}{4}$ | $16\frac{9}{16}$ | 3.69 |
| $9\frac{1}{2}$ | 14 | $18\frac{7}{8}$ | $\frac{3}{4}$ | $17\frac{1}{8}$ | 3.81 |
| 10 | 16 | $19\frac{3}{8}$ | $\frac{3}{4}$ | $17\frac{5}{8}$ | 3.44 |
| 11 | 16 | $19\frac{7}{8}$ | $\frac{3}{4}$ | $18\frac{1}{8}$ | 3.54 |
| 12 | 16 | 21 | $\frac{3}{4}$ | $19\frac{1}{4}$ | 3.75 |

TABLE X.—BUREAU OF ENGINEERING—HIGH-PRESSURE BULKHEAD FLANGES, NAVY STANDARD

| Size | No. of holes | Diam. | Size of bolt | Pitch circle | Pitch chord |
|------|------|------|------|------|------|
| ¼ | 8 | 6¾ | ½ | 5½ | 2.10 |
| ½ | 8 | 7 | ½ | 5¾ | 2.20 |
| ¾ | 8 | 7⅜ | ½ | 6⅛ | 2.34 |
| 1 | 8 | 8⅛ | ½ | 6⅞ | 2.63 |
| 1¼ | 10 | 8⅜ | ½ | 7⅛ | 2.20 |
| 1½ | 10 | 9 | ½ | 7¾ | 2.39 |
| 2 | 10 | 10¼ | ⅝ | 8¾ | 2.70 |
| 2½ | 10 | 11⅜ | ⅝ | 9⅞ | 3.05 |
| 3 | 10 | 11⅞ | ⅝ | 10⅜ | 3.21 |
| 3½ | 12 | 12½ | ⅝ | 11 | 2.85 |
| 4 | 12 | 13 | ⅝ | 11½ | 2.98 |
| 4½ | 12 | 13⅝ | ⅝ | 12⅛ | 3.14 |
| 5 | 12 | 14⅛ | ⅝ | 12⅝ | 3.27 |
| 5½ | 12 | 15¾ | ¾ | 14 | 3.62 |
| 6 | 12 | 16⅜ | ¾ | 14⅝ | 3.79 |
| 6½ | 14 | 17 | ¾ | 15¼ | 3.39 |
| 7 | 14 | 17½ | ¾ | 15¾ | 3.50 |
| 7½ | 14 | 18⅝ | ¾ | 16⅞ | 3.76 |
| 8 | 16 | 19⅛ | ¾ | 17⅜ | 3.39 |
| 8½ | 16 | 19¾ | ¾ | 18 | 3.51 |
| 9 | 16 | 20¼ | ¾ | 18½ | 3.61 |
| 9½ | 16 | 20⅞ | ¾ | 19⅛ | 3.73 |
| 10 | 18 | 21⅜ | ¾ | 19⅝ | 3.41 |
| 10½ | 18 | 22 | ¾ | 20¼ | 3.52 |
| 11 | 18 | 23 | ¾ | 21¼ | 3.69 |
| 11½ | 18 | 23½ | ¾ | 21¾ | 3.78 |
| 12 | 18 | 24⅛ | ¾ | 22⅜ | 3.88 |

*MARINE COPPERSMITHING*

TABLE XI.—Bureau of Engineering—Standard Low-pressure Flanges, Navy Standard

| Size | No. of holes | Diam. | Size of bolt | Pitch circle |
|---|---|---|---|---|
| $\frac{1}{4}$ | 3 | $3\frac{1}{4}$ | $\frac{1}{2}$ | $2\frac{1}{8}$ |
| $\frac{1}{2}$ | 3 | $3\frac{9}{16}$ | $\frac{1}{2}$ | $2\frac{7}{16}$ |
| $\frac{3}{4}$ | 4 | $3\frac{13}{16}$ | $\frac{1}{2}$ | $2\frac{11}{16}$ |
| 1 | 4 | $4\frac{1}{4}$ | $\frac{1}{2}$ | $3\frac{1}{8}$ |
| $1\frac{1}{4}$ | 4 | $4\frac{1}{2}$ | $\frac{1}{2}$ | $3\frac{3}{8}$ |
| $1\frac{1}{2}$ | 6 | $5\frac{1}{16}$ | $\frac{1}{2}$ | $3\frac{15}{16}$ |
| 2 | 6 | $5\frac{9}{16}$ | $\frac{1}{2}$ | $4\frac{7}{16}$ |
| $2\frac{1}{2}$ | 6 | $6\frac{1}{8}$ | $\frac{1}{2}$ | 5 |
| 3 | 8 | $6\frac{5}{8}$ | $\frac{1}{2}$ | $5\frac{1}{2}$ |
| $3\frac{1}{2}$ | 8 | $7\frac{3}{16}$ | $\frac{1}{2}$ | $6\frac{1}{16}$ |
| 4 | 8 | $7\frac{11}{16}$ | $\frac{1}{2}$ | $6\frac{9}{16}$ |
| $4\frac{1}{2}$ | 10 | $8\frac{3}{16}$ | $\frac{1}{2}$ | $7\frac{1}{16}$ |
| 5 | 10 | $9\frac{1}{16}$ | $\frac{5}{8}$ | $7\frac{13}{16}$ |
| $5\frac{1}{2}$ | 10 | $9\frac{9}{16}$ | $\frac{5}{8}$ | $8\frac{5}{16}$ |
| 6 | 12 | $10\frac{1}{8}$ | $\frac{5}{8}$ | $8\frac{7}{8}$ |
| $6\frac{1}{2}$ | 12 | $10\frac{5}{8}$ | $\frac{5}{8}$ | $9\frac{3}{8}$ |
| 7 | 12 | $11\frac{5}{16}$ | $\frac{5}{8}$ | 10 |
| $7\frac{1}{2}$ | 12 | $11\frac{7}{8}$ | $\frac{5}{8}$ | $10\frac{9}{16}$ |
| 8 | 14 | $12\frac{3}{8}$ | $\frac{5}{8}$ | $11\frac{1}{16}$ |
| $8\frac{1}{2}$ | 14 | $12\frac{15}{16}$ | $\frac{5}{8}$ | $11\frac{5}{8}$ |
| 9 | 14 | $13\frac{15}{16}$ | $\frac{3}{4}$ | $12\frac{3}{8}$ |
| $9\frac{1}{2}$ | 14 | $14\frac{1}{2}$ | $\frac{3}{4}$ | $12\frac{15}{16}$ |
| 10 | 15 | 15 | $\frac{3}{4}$ | $13\frac{7}{16}$ |
| 11 | 15 | $15\frac{1}{2}$ | $\frac{3}{4}$ | $13\frac{15}{16}$ |
| 12 | 16 | $16\frac{9}{16}$ | $\frac{3}{4}$ | 15 |

TABLE XII.—BUREAU OF ENGINEERING—STANDARD HIGH-PRESSURE FLANGES, NAVY STANDARD

| Size | No. of holes | Diam. | Size of bolt | Pitch circle |
|------|------|------|------|------|
| $\frac{1}{4}$ | 3 | $3\frac{3}{4}$ | $\frac{1}{2}$ | $2\frac{5}{8}$ |
| $\frac{1}{2}$ | 4 | 4 | $\frac{1}{2}$ | $2\frac{7}{8}$ |
| $\frac{3}{4}$ | 4 | $4\frac{5}{16}$ | $\frac{1}{2}$ | $3\frac{3}{16}$ |
| 1 | 5 | $5\frac{1}{16}$ | $\frac{5}{8}$ | $3\frac{3}{4}$ |
| $1\frac{1}{4}$ | 5 | $5\frac{3}{8}$ | $\frac{5}{8}$ | $4\frac{1}{16}$ |
| $1\frac{1}{2}$ | 6 | $5\frac{15}{16}$ | $\frac{5}{8}$ | $4\frac{5}{8}$ |
| 2 | 7 | $6\frac{1}{2}$ | $\frac{5}{8}$ | $5\frac{3}{16}$ |
| $2\frac{1}{2}$ | 8 | $7\frac{9}{16}$ | $\frac{3}{4}$ | 6 |
| 3 | 8 | $8\frac{1}{8}$ | $\frac{3}{4}$ | $6\frac{9}{16}$ |
| $3\frac{1}{2}$ | 9 | $8\frac{11}{16}$ | $\frac{3}{4}$ | $7\frac{1}{8}$ |
| 4 | 9 | $9\frac{1}{4}$ | $\frac{3}{4}$ | $7\frac{11}{16}$ |
| $4\frac{1}{2}$ | 10 | $9\frac{13}{16}$ | $\frac{3}{4}$ | $8\frac{1}{4}$ |
| 5 | 11 | $10\frac{3}{8}$ | $\frac{3}{4}$ | $8\frac{13}{16}$ |
| $5\frac{1}{2}$ | 11 | $11\frac{3}{8}$ | $\frac{7}{8}$ | $9\frac{5}{8}$ |
| 6 | 12 | $11\frac{15}{16}$ | $\frac{7}{8}$ | $10\frac{3}{16}$ |
| $6\frac{1}{2}$ | 12 | $12\frac{9}{16}$ | $\frac{7}{8}$ | $10\frac{13}{16}$ |
| 7 | 12 | $13\frac{1}{8}$ | $\frac{7}{8}$ | $11\frac{3}{8}$ |
| $7\frac{1}{2}$ | 12 | $14\frac{3}{16}$ | 1 | $12\frac{3}{16}$ |
| 8 | 13 | $14\frac{3}{4}$ | 1 | $12\frac{3}{4}$ |
| $8\frac{1}{2}$ | 13 | $15\frac{5}{16}$ | 1 | $13\frac{5}{16}$ |
| 9 | 14 | $15\frac{7}{8}$ | 1 | $13\frac{7}{8}$ |
| $9\frac{1}{2}$ | 15 | $16\frac{7}{16}$ | 1 | $14\frac{7}{16}$ |
| 10 | 15 | 17 | 1 | 15 |
| $10\frac{1}{2}$ | 15 | $17\frac{9}{16}$ | 1 | $15\frac{9}{16}$ |
| 11 | 15 | $18\frac{9}{16}$ | $1\frac{1}{8}$ | $16\frac{3}{8}$ |
| $11\frac{1}{2}$ | 16 | $19\frac{1}{8}$ | $1\frac{1}{8}$ | $16\frac{15}{16}$ |
| 12 | 16 | $19\frac{3}{4}$ | $1\frac{1}{8}$ | $17\frac{9}{16}$ |
| 13 | 18 | $20\frac{7}{8}$ | $1\frac{1}{8}$ | $18\frac{11}{16}$ |

TABLE XIII.—CONSTRUCTION AND REPAIR FLANGES, NAVY STANDARD

| Size | No. of holes | Diam. | Size of bolt | Pitch circle |
|---|---|---|---|---|
| $\frac{1}{2}$ | 3 | $3\frac{9}{16}$ | $\frac{1}{2}$ | $2\frac{7}{16}$ |
| $\frac{3}{4}$ | 4 | $3\frac{13}{16}$ | $\frac{1}{2}$ | $2\frac{11}{16}$ |
| 1 | 4 | $4\frac{1}{4}$ | $\frac{1}{2}$ | $3\frac{1}{8}$ |
| $1\frac{1}{4}$ | 4 | $4\frac{1}{2}$ | $\frac{1}{2}$ | $3\frac{3}{8}$ |
| $1\frac{1}{2}$ | 6 | $5\frac{1}{16}$ | $\frac{1}{2}$ | $3\frac{15}{16}$ |
| 2 | 6 | $5\frac{9}{16}$ | $\frac{1}{2}$ | $4\frac{7}{16}$ |
| $2\frac{1}{2}$ | 6 | $6\frac{1}{8}$ | $\frac{1}{2}$ | 5 |
| 3 | 8 | $6\frac{5}{8}$ | $\frac{1}{2}$ | $5\frac{1}{2}$ |
| $3\frac{1}{2}$ | 8 | $7\frac{3}{16}$ | $\frac{1}{2}$ | $6\frac{1}{16}$ |
| 4 | 8 | $7\frac{11}{16}$ | $\frac{1}{2}$ | $6\frac{9}{16}$ |
| $4\frac{1}{2}$ | 10 | $8\frac{3}{16}$ | $\frac{1}{2}$ | $7\frac{1}{16}$ |
| 5 | 10 | $9\frac{1}{16}$ | $\frac{5}{8}$ | $7\frac{13}{16}$ |
| $5\frac{1}{2}$ | 10 | $9\frac{9}{16}$ | $\frac{5}{8}$ | $8\frac{5}{16}$ |
| 6 | 12 | $10\frac{1}{8}$ | $\frac{5}{8}$ | $8\frac{7}{8}$ |
| $6\frac{1}{2}$ | 12 | $10\frac{5}{8}$ | $\frac{5}{8}$ | $9\frac{3}{8}$ |
| 7 | 12 | $11\frac{5}{16}$ | $\frac{5}{8}$ | 10 |
| $7\frac{1}{2}$ | 12 | $11\frac{7}{8}$ | $\frac{5}{8}$ | $10\frac{9}{16}$ |
| 8 | 14 | $12\frac{3}{8}$ | $\frac{5}{8}$ | $11\frac{1}{16}$ |
| $8\frac{1}{2}$ | 14 | $12\frac{15}{16}$ | $\frac{5}{8}$ | $11\frac{5}{8}$ |
| 9 | 14 | $13\frac{15}{16}$ | $\frac{3}{4}$ | $12\frac{3}{8}$ |
| $9\frac{1}{2}$ | 14 | $14\frac{1}{2}$ | $\frac{3}{4}$ | $12\frac{15}{16}$ |
| 10 | 15 | 15 | $\frac{3}{4}$ | $13\frac{7}{16}$ |
| $10\frac{1}{2}$ | 15 | $15\frac{1}{2}$ | $\frac{3}{4}$ | $13\frac{15}{16}$ |
| 11 | 15 | 16 | $\frac{3}{4}$ | $14\frac{7}{16}$ |
| $11\frac{1}{2}$ | 16 | $16\frac{9}{16}$ | $\frac{3}{4}$ | 15 |
| 12 | 16 | $17\frac{1}{8}$ | $\frac{3}{4}$ | $15\frac{1}{2}$ |
| $12\frac{1}{2}$ | 18 | $17\frac{5}{8}$ | $\frac{3}{4}$ | $16\frac{1}{16}$ |
| 13 | 18 | $18\frac{3}{8}$ | $\frac{3}{4}$ | $16\frac{3}{4}$ |

### TABLE XIV.—DECIMAL EQUIVALENTS

| | | | | | | | | |
|---|---|---|---|---|---|---|---|---|
| | $\frac{1}{64}$ | 0.0156 | | $\frac{11}{32}$ | 0.3437 | | $\frac{43}{64}$ | 0.6718 |
| | $\frac{1}{32}$ | 0.0312 | | $\frac{23}{64}$ | 0.3593 | $\frac{11}{16}$ | | 0.6875 |
| | $\frac{3}{64}$ | 0.0468 | $\frac{3}{8}$ | | 0.375 | | $\frac{45}{64}$ | 0.7031 |
| $\frac{1}{16}$ | | 0.0625 | | $\frac{25}{64}$ | 0.3906 | | $\frac{23}{32}$ | 0.7187 |
| | $\frac{5}{64}$ | 0.0781 | | $\frac{13}{32}$ | 0.4062 | | $\frac{47}{64}$ | 0.7343 |
| | $\frac{3}{32}$ | 0.0937 | | $\frac{27}{64}$ | 0.4218 | $\frac{3}{4}$ | | 0.75 |
| | $\frac{7}{64}$ | 0.1093 | $\frac{7}{16}$ | | 0.4375 | | $\frac{49}{64}$ | 0.7656 |
| $\frac{1}{8}$ | | 0.125 | | $\frac{29}{64}$ | 0.4531 | | $\frac{25}{32}$ | 0.7812 |
| | $\frac{9}{64}$ | 0.1406 | | $\frac{15}{32}$ | 0.4687 | | $\frac{51}{64}$ | 0.7968 |
| | $\frac{5}{32}$ | 0.1562 | | $\frac{31}{64}$ | 0.4843 | $\frac{13}{16}$ | | 0.8125 |
| | $\frac{11}{64}$ | 0.1718 | $\frac{1}{2}$ | | 0.5 | | $\frac{53}{64}$ | 0.8281 |
| $\frac{3}{16}$ | | 0.1875 | | $\frac{33}{64}$ | 0.5156 | | $\frac{27}{32}$ | 0.8437 |
| | $\frac{13}{64}$ | 0.2031 | | $\frac{17}{32}$ | 0.5312 | | $\frac{55}{64}$ | 0.8593 |
| | $\frac{7}{32}$ | 0.2187 | | $\frac{35}{64}$ | 0.5468 | $\frac{7}{8}$ | | 0.875 |
| | $\frac{15}{64}$ | 0.2343 | $\frac{9}{16}$ | | 0.5625 | | $\frac{57}{64}$ | 0.8906 |
| $\frac{1}{4}$ | | 0.25 | | $\frac{37}{64}$ | 0.5781 | | $\frac{29}{32}$ | 0.9062 |
| | $\frac{17}{64}$ | 0.2656 | | $\frac{19}{32}$ | 0.5937 | | $\frac{59}{64}$ | 0.9218 |
| | $\frac{9}{32}$ | 0.2812 | | $\frac{39}{64}$ | 0.6093 | $\frac{15}{16}$ | | 0.9375 |
| | $\frac{19}{64}$ | 0.2968 | $\frac{5}{8}$ | | 0.625 | | $\frac{61}{64}$ | 0.9531 |
| $\frac{5}{16}$ | | 0.3125 | | $\frac{41}{64}$ | 0.6406 | | $\frac{31}{32}$ | 0.9687 |
| | $\frac{21}{64}$ | 0.3281 | | $\frac{21}{32}$ | 0.6562 | | $\frac{63}{64}$ | 0.9843 |

## TABLE XV.—STANDARD PIPE*

| Size, I.P.S., in. | Actual O.D., decimals, in. | O.D., fractions, in. | Thread per in. | Tap-drill size, in. | Clearance drill size, in. | Silver-solder fit, in. |
|---|---|---|---|---|---|---|
| $\frac{1}{8}$ | 0.405 | $\frac{13}{32}$ | 27 | $1\frac{1}{32}$ | $\frac{27}{64}$ | $1\frac{3}{32}$ |
| $\frac{1}{4}$ | 0.540 | $\frac{17}{32}$ | 18 | $\frac{7}{16}$ | $\frac{9}{16}$ | $\frac{35}{64}$ |
| $\frac{3}{8}$ | 0.675 | $\frac{21}{32}$ | 18 | $\frac{37}{64}$ | $1\frac{1}{16}$ | $\frac{43}{64}$ |
| $\frac{1}{2}$ | 0.840 | $\frac{27}{32}$ | 14 | $\frac{45}{64}$ | $\frac{55}{64}$ | $\frac{27}{32}$ |
| $\frac{3}{4}$ | 1.050 | $1\frac{1}{16}$ | 14 | $\frac{59}{64}$ | $1\frac{1}{16}$ | $1\frac{3}{64}$ |
| 1 | 1.315 | $1\frac{5}{16}$ | $11\frac{1}{2}$ | $1\frac{9}{64}$ | $1\frac{21}{64}$ | $1\frac{5}{16}$ |
| $1\frac{1}{4}$ | 1.660 | $1\frac{21}{32}$ | $11\frac{1}{2}$ | $1\frac{33}{64}$ | $1\frac{43}{64}$ | $1\frac{21}{32}$ |
| $1\frac{1}{2}$ | 1.900 | $1\frac{29}{32}$ | $11\frac{1}{2}$ | $1\frac{3}{4}$ | $1\frac{59}{64}$ | $1\frac{29}{32}$ |
| 2 | 2.375 | $2\frac{3}{8}$ | $11\frac{1}{2}$ | $2\frac{13}{64}$ | $2\frac{25}{64}$ | $2\frac{3}{8}$ |
| $2\frac{1}{2}$ | 2.875 | $2\frac{7}{8}$ | 8 | $2\frac{5}{8}$ | $2\frac{29}{32}$ | $2\frac{57}{64}$ |
| 3 | 3.500 | $3\frac{1}{2}$ | | | | |
| $3\frac{1}{2}$ | 4.000 | 4 | | | | |
| 4 | 4.500 | $4\frac{1}{2}$ | | | | |
| $4\frac{1}{2}$ | 5.000 | 5 | | | | |
| 5 | 5.563 | $5\frac{9}{16}$ | | | | |
| $5\frac{1}{2}$ | 6.125 | $6\frac{1}{8}$ | | | | |
| 6 | 6.625 | $6\frac{5}{8}$ | | | | |
| $6\frac{1}{2}$ | 7.125 | $7\frac{1}{8}$ | | | | |
| 7 | 7.625 | $7\frac{5}{8}$ | | | | |
| $7\frac{1}{2}$ | 8.125 | $8\frac{1}{8}$ | | | | |
| 8 | 8.625 | $8\frac{5}{8}$ | | | | |
| $8\frac{1}{2}$ | 9.125 | $9\frac{1}{8}$ | | | | |
| 9 | 9.625 | $9\frac{5}{8}$ | | | | |
| $9\frac{1}{2}$ | 10.250 | $10\frac{1}{4}$ | | | | |
| 10 | 10.75 | $10\frac{3}{4}$ | | | | |
| $10\frac{1}{2}$ | 11.250 | $11\frac{1}{4}$ | | | | |
| 11 | 11.75 | $11\frac{3}{4}$ | | | | |
| $11\frac{1}{2}$ | 12.250 | $12\frac{1}{4}$ | | | | |
| 12 | 12.75 | $12\frac{3}{4}$ | | | | |

* Standard pipe threads are tapered $\frac{3}{4}$ in. per ft.

# CHAPTER VIII

## REDUCING A PIPE AND MAKING A CUP JOINT

### A. REDUCING COPPER PIPE

In pipe-fitting work, whenever it is necessary to make a reduction in a steel or brass pipe line, a cast or machined reducing fitting is used. This is not necessary when working with copper pipe, as the copper can easily be worked to the desired reduction with simple tools and heat. However, fittings can be used on copper lines also, but, since streamlined jobs are usually preferred, the reduction is made by hammering the pipe to the required size.

Figure 15 shows the method of reducing a copper pipe. Anneal the pipe, lay it on a grooved wooden horse or swage block, and hammer with a wooden mallet, as illustrated in Fig. 15A. Keep revolving the pipe while hammering. The pipe should be revolved in opposite directions after each annealing, to keep the reduction on center. If the pipe were revolved in one direction only, there would be a tendency for the reduction to become off-center. Start the reducing operation by hammering lightly away from the end at the shoulder and work toward the end. As the pipe is hammered, wrinkles will appear. While the pipe rests on a steel bar, these wrinkles should be smoothed by use of a steel hammer on the outside of the pipe (see Fig. 15B).

The pipe should be annealed after each hammering operation. The number of annealings necessary to make the entire reduction depends on the amount of reduction being made during each annealing and on the total amount of reduction to be completed. Copper-nickel-alloy pipe must be reduced while it is cold because it will break if reduced while in a heated state. Otherwise it is worked like copper and must be annealed between stages.

Figure 15C, shows the final finishing of the reduced pipe; the shoulder is being rounded with a hammer and bar. The taper of the shoulder itself depends very much on the local situation and on the depth of the reduction. Usually about a 45 deg. angle is sufficient.

69

A steel swage block is shown in Fig. 15D. This is used for reducing small-diameter tubing. The part of the tube to be

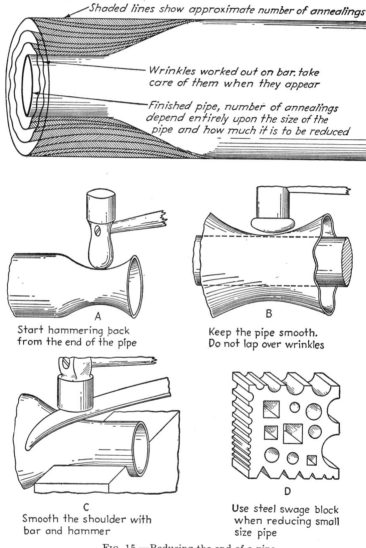

Shaded lines show approximate number of annealings

Wrinkles worked out on bar. take care of them when they appear

Finished pipe, number of annealings depend entirely upon the size of the pipe and how much it is to be reduced

A
Start hammering back from the end of the pipe

B
Keep the pipe smooth. Do not lap over wrinkles

C
Smooth the shoulder with bar and hammer

D
Use steel swage block when reducing small size pipe

FIG. 15.—Reducing the end of a pipe.

reduced is laid in the grooves of the steel swage block and hammered while being turned. As it gradually becomes smaller, place it in the smaller grooves of the swage block. A wooden mallet and a steel hammer may be used while reducing the tube, starting with the mallet while the copper is hot. The hammer blows should be light at first because heavy hammering will cause wrinkles to form more quickly.

The swage block is best for working small-diameter tubing. It is much faster because of the steel backing. Each blow of the hammer is backed by the steel block, so that the copper receives the full benefit of the hammer's weight.

## B. CUP JOINTS

A cup joint is a type of connection in which two sections of pipe are joined together without the aid of flanges, couplings, or sleeves. The cup joint has great possibilities, especially when flanges and cast couplings may be difficult to obtain. The copper tube of one section is expanded to receive the other section of pipe, and the two sections are then spelter brazed or silver brazed together, resulting in a durable joint manufactured on the spot.

The cup joint can be used wherever silver-solder couplings or flanges have been used, and sometimes it is used where flanges cannot be placed, such as on coils or in tight places aboard ship. Whenever weight is an important factor and removability is not necessary, the cup joints may be used because they are much lighter than flanges.

The cup may be expanded either by the hand method, which calls for a hammer and a steel bar, or with a tube expander. Either method is satisfactory on small tubing, but on large sizes of pipe the cup may be made by direct hammering against the inside of the pipe with a round-nosed wooden mallet or a long-nosed bumping hammer.

If the joint is to be spelter brazed, a lip is turned over at the top of the cup to hold the spelter grains during the brazing operation. The object is not just to fill the lip with spelter but to let it penetrate deeply into the cup. If only the lip were filled, without the spelter penetrating deeper, the joint would be weak and might develop leaks. However, when the job is done, the lip should be full of spelter and the surface should be smooth; no rough places or pinholes should be visible.

When the joint is being silver brazed, the spelter lip is not necessary because silver solder is generally in rod form and can be applied with ease.

**Operations.**—The operations involved in the manufacture of a cup joint are very simple and can be done with the simplest tools.

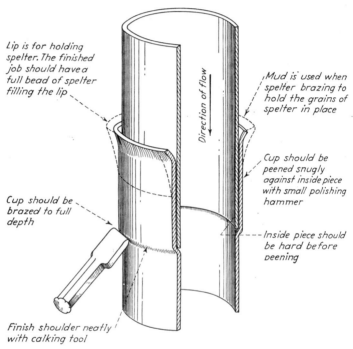

Lip is for holding spelter. The finished job should have a full bead of spelter filling the lip

Direction of flow

Mud is used when spelter brazing to hold the grains of spelter in place

Cup should be peened snugly against inside piece with small polishing hammer

Cup should be brazed to full depth

Inside piece should be hard before peening

Finish shoulder neatly with calking tool

Fɪɢ. 16.—Cup joint. The depth of the cup is equal to the diameter of the pipe up to 5 in. In larger sizes the depth of the cup is very seldom over 8 or 9 in. If the cup joint is to be silver brazed, the lip at the top of the collar is not necessary.

Only a hammer and a 1-in. round bar are necessary besides heat and spelter or silver alloy.

Start the operations by annealing the pipe that is to be cupped. Lay the annealed pipe on a grooved wooden horse, insert a 1-in. steel bar into the end of the pipe to the depth of the desired cup, and strike it with a hammer while the pipe is being turned. Keep hammering until the copper has hardened or until the pipe has expanded enough. When the copper has hardened, anneal it again and repeat the operation. When the cup has expanded enough to allow the inside piece to enter, turn the lip as shown in Fig. 16. Use a square-shouldered piece of iron as a backing while turning the lip. Anneal and clean the cup. If it is not

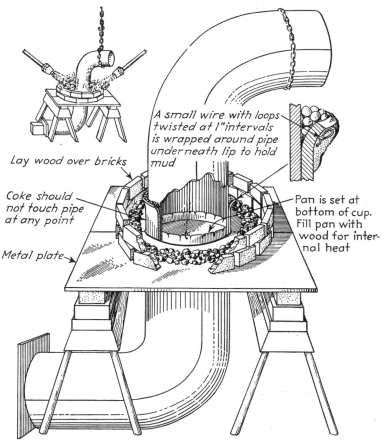

A small wire with loops twisted at 1"intervals is wrapped around pipe underneath lip to hold mud

Lay wood over bricks

Coke should not touch pipe at any point

Metal plate

Pan is set at bottom of cup. Fill pan with wood for internal heat

Mud should be placed on seams both inside and outside of pipe
No drafts should be allowed to come through
Hammered seams will not melt out as quickly as unhammered seams

Fig. 17.—Brazing setup, large cup joint.

already hard, the pipe that is to be placed inside should be hardened before the final insertion. Clean the inside piece, fit the two together, and then calk the cup tightly against the hard inside piece. When it is calked solidly, pour borax water into the cup; tap it to make the borax water go down between the cup and the inside piece.   Then set up the pipe for brazing, level it, and place fire clay under the lip, as shown in Fig. 17, to make a ledge for holding spelter grains.   Arrange a few firebricks and wood as backing, heat the cup, and then braze.   Try to flow the spelter deeply into the cup by heating thoroughly, filling the lip a second time with spelter if necessary, and finishing a full, smooth shoulder.   Care should be taken that no lumps or pin-holes are visible in the finished braze.

When the cup joint is to be silver brazed, the cup and inside piece should be fluxed with silver-solder flux before the insertion and the peening.

**Large Cup Joint.**—It is necessary sometimes to make a cup joint in a large pipe that has been made of sheet copper.   The method used is much the same as that employed for a small cup joint, except that the proportion changes for the depth of the cup when the larger sizes are being worked.   A cup is seldom over 8 or 10 in. deep, even on large diameters.   A depth of from 8 to 10 in. is sufficient for a cup on pipes up to 20 in. in diameter or more.

**Peening and Fitting.**—The cup is made to fit the companion piece, and then the lip is turned.   After both pieces have been cleaned, they are fitted together and calked.   The calking, which is done with any suitable planishing or ball-peen hammer, should be as snug as possible.   If the fit is very loose, the pieces should first be set up with a wooden mallet before being calked with a steel hammer.

The foundation for the brazier is made of steel plates or sheet metal, which should be fitted closely against the pipe.   All cracks and openings between the plate and the pipe should be filled with fire clay.   Large work of this type is best heated with two large torches working on opposite sides.   The flame is played upon the cup and coke, heating as large a surface as possible.   After the spelter once melts, it is often necessary to fill the spelter trough a second time.   During the second heating, the heat should be kept higher so that the spelter will not run through.   A good setup will save time, and a good smooth job will be the result.

**Always raise the torch in the air vertically when not actually brazing.   Never swing the torch around horizontally or turn it toward the floor.**

**Setup.**—The setup for brazing is very important in every detail. The bottom end of the pipe should be blanked off to keep the draft from coming through; this may be done by laying a pan in the pipe just below the cup or by plugging the bottom end with a plate. This inside pan should also be filled with wood to aid in heating the cup during brazing. Enough wood should be placed inside the pipe to fill it well above the cup itself.

A brazier is built around the cup at the outside, to the height of the cup. Coke is laid so that it does not touch the pipe; about 2 in. clearance is desirable between the coke and the pipe (see Fig. 17).

**Mudding.**—Tinker's clay, a mixture of equal parts of fire clay, fine sand, and asbestos, plus water, is placed on the seams, both inside and outside the pipe, to prevent the spelter from melting in the seam while the cup is being brazed. Mud is also placed at the lip of the cup, making a dam to hold the spelter while brazing. The mud at the lip is reinforced by a wire that is made with loops about 1 in. apart. The looped wire is wrapped around under the lip; the mud is placed on the wire and smoothed out, leaving a trough for the spelter to lie in. (See detailed cut in Fig. 17.)

**Large Cup Joint, Silver Brazed.**—The large cup joint may also be silver brazed as well as spelter brazed, and when there is need for speed, silver brazing is the logical method. The setup for silver brazing is much simpler than that for spelter brazing, and the lip on the collar is unnecessary. Silver brazing may be done in any convenient position, because silver in rod form is easily handled. The capillary action of heat on silver solder draws the silver uphill as well as downhill, provided that the fits are made with close tolerances.

Preheating of the cup may be done with a large kerosene or gas torch and finished with an acetylene torch. Always set up a few pieces of wood or a backing of bricks to intensify the heat around the cup, in a manner similar to the spelter brazing setup. This will save heat and also control it.

# CHAPTER IX

## BRANCHES

A coppersmith need not resort to the use of manufactured cast fittings each time that a fitting or a tee is needed. Delays in the manufacture and delivery of these fittings need not occur if the coppersmith were allowed to follow his own resourcefulness. Little, if any, short ends of copper tubing should be discarded. Lengths as short as 6 in. can be made into branches and stored in stock. Standard copper tee fittings can easily be made from these short ends, relieving the pressure on the pattern shop, foundry, and machine shop during times when they are overloaded with work.

Cast tee fittings are about twice the weight of the copper branch, and, when fitted to copper lines, they are an unnecessary bulk. There are times, of course, when the quick separation of a joint is necessary; the use of these fittings then is advisable. The present great use of tees, however, may have been caused largely both by high-pressure advertising and by a lack of understanding of coppersmithing possibilities by engineers and draftsmen.

Placing a branch instead of a tee fitting in a line eliminates not only excessive weight but also at least one extra pair of flanges. Saving material and expense has always been good practice, whether during peace or war, and a pair of flanges saved means valuable material saved.

**Branches.**—Generally speaking, there are two types of branches, namely, the "cup" branch and the "saddle" branch; the cup branch with reinforcing collar and the inside-brazed cup branches are merely variations of the cup branch. The advantage of the branch is that it can be placed at any angle or in any position on a pipe. It may be placed either on the side, in the back, or in the throat of bends. A well-made and well-brazed branch is just as strong as the pipe itself. It will stand vibration and pressure. Branches are light in weight, and, wherever weight is a factor to be considered, it is logical to use branches.

**Cup Branch.**—The cup branch is very widely used in marine coppersmithing. It is easy and quick to make, as is seen from Fig. 18. It is easy to braze if reasonable care is taken in fitting and calking. The branch should be brazed to the full depth of the cup, not merely at the top of the lip.

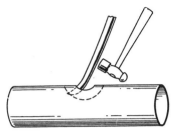

Drill a small hole at center of spot to be worked. Anneal the pipe after drilling. Use a raising bar to lift the copper

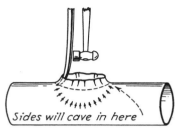

The sides will cave in when raising the opening. They should be bumped out with a ball, or the rounded end of a raising bar

When copper is raised. A lip is bent over to hold spelter. Note: The lip is not necessary if job is to be silver brazed

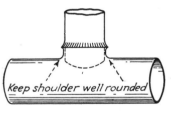

The pipe is inserted into the hole and calked with calking tool. After brazing if spelter brazed, the lip should not be removed

FIG. 18.—Steps in making a cup branch.

Sometimes the direction of the flow is the deciding factor in whether a cup or saddle branch is used. When used on plumbing lines, it is important that no shoulder or edge be left inside to obstruct the passage. In this case cup branches have an advantage over saddle branches because the flow from the branch to the main line is not interrupted. Branches are made of copper or copper-nickel alloys.

**Steps in Making a Cup Branch** (see Fig. 18).—Locate the point where the branch is to be fitted and then drill a hole. When drilling, always make the hole small to compensate for the loss of metal due to raising the shoulder.   After the hole has been drilled, the section to be raised is annealed.   As much raising as possible is done while the metal is still red-hot.   Keep hammering against the raising bar while raising the complete diameter of the hole.   Keep the hole as nearly round as possible, and keep it smooth.   If allowed to become rough and dented, it will have to be smoothed, adding an unnecessary operation to the job.

When opened sufficiently to fit the branch pipe, a spelter lip may be turned at the top of the collar.   This lip is necessary only in spelter brazing, because of the use of spelter in the grain form. Brazing with a bronze or silver rod makes the lip unnecessary.

Before the branch pipe is inserted for peening and brazing, it should be hardened and cleaned.   The part to be fitted should be trimmed to fit the pipe's inside contour, allowing free flow. After the branch is cut to fit the contour, it should be thin-edged about $\frac{3}{8}$ to $\frac{1}{2}$ in. from the end.   This will partially do away with the abrupt shoulder inside.

When both parts are clean and ready, the branch is set in the opening and peened in with calking tools.   When peening, hold a hand dolly or suitable backing tool at the opposite side from the side being peened, to absorb the jar.

In setting up for brazing, whether spelter or silver brazing, it is necessary to rig a small flat bar, fastening it to the branch and the pipe to prevent the branch from falling into the pipe when the heat expands the cup that is being brazed.   After brazing, set the inside edge tightly against the side of the pipe, thus ensuring a smooth interior surface.

**Raising a Cup Branch, Bumping Method** (see Fig. 19).— When working a cup branch into a large pipe, the method of bumping from the inside is recommended because it is quicker and easier to do.   Bumping can bring more metal to the collar (if needed) than can raising the metal with a raising bar.

Locate the spot where the hole is needed, heat the metal to a red heat, and then bump it, keeping the copper red-hot during the bumping operation.   When the necessary height is reached, cut the hole, opening the pipe.   The hole is cut by using a small drill, $\frac{3}{16}$ or $\frac{1}{4}$ in., and drilling a ring of small holes, one tight against the other, until the complete circle is drilled. The piece may be removed by striking it with a hammer or by cutting with a chisel the small sections that may still be holding. File away all rough edges of the opening before attempting further to work the copper.

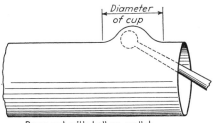

Bump out with ball or mallet

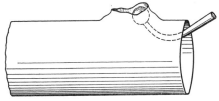

Cut hole in top and work out sides

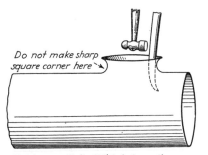

Finish cup with lip if it is to be spelter brazed. Lip unnecessary for silver brazing

Fig. 19.—Making a cup branch, bump method.

**Copper Saddle Branches.**—Saddle branches are made by the coppersmith of either copper or copper-nickel alloys. The saddle is a very satisfactory branch, since it is strong and can be fitted with ease onto the bends, the throat, or the back of pipe and at angles.

The saddle branch can be made to accommodate the flow of liquid and sewage in either direction, provided that a short branch is used. In order to prevent any projections on the interior of the pipe, smooth the inside copper tightly against the

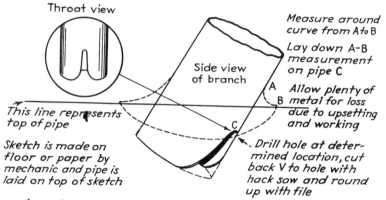

Throat view

Side view
of branch

This line represents
top of pipe

Sketch is made on
floor or paper by
mechanic and pipe is
laid on top of sketch

Measure around
curve from A to B

Lay down A-B
measurement
on pipe C

Allow plenty of
metal for loss
due to upsetting
and working

Drill hole at deter-
mined location, cut
back V to hole with
hack saw and round
up with file

Important :- Allow more metal than is needed, you can
always trim where necessary

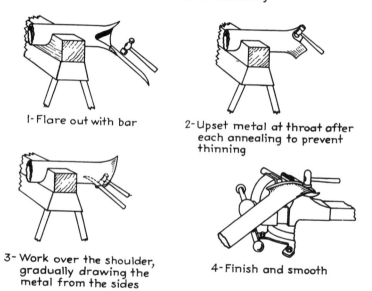

1-Flare out with bar

2-Upset metal at throat after
each annealing to prevent
thinning

3- Work over the shoulder,
gradually drawing the
metal from the sides

4-Finish and smooth

Fig. 20.—Making an angle saddle branch.

branch with a raising bar and fill the lap with silver solder or spelter.

**Working the Angle Saddle Branch.**—Figure 20 shows annealed pipe being flared out with a bar while the pipe is held in a grooved notch on a wooden horse. The sides should be flared out considerably, but the back and throat are stretched just enough to keep the pipe from caving in. The metal at the throat or *V* should be upset after each annealing, in the manner shown in part 2. A 3-in. branch may have to be annealed about a half dozen times before it is completed.

When the sides are flared out an exaggerated distance, they should be hammered toward the throat to allow metal for the turnover at the throat without stretching or thinning. Do not allow the branch to become too greatly distorted. Try to keep it somewhere near the shape that it will have when it is completed.

Part 3 shows the metal being driven back to shape the throat part. If the sides are thoroughly stretched and the metal is driven properly toward the throat, there is very little thinning of metal at the throat. Part 4 shows final shaping up, just before placing the branch on a pipe to check for the angle. The proper angle adjustment can be made either by working the throat more or by adjusting the toe to get the desired angle.

**Right-angle Saddle Branch.**—In making a saddle branch that is to be placed at a 90-deg., or right, angle to the pipe to which it is to be fitted, the following operations are performed. Square the end, and then bell the pipe by placing it in a grooved wooden horse and hammering it in the same manner as shown in Fig. 20, part 1. Anneal it as many times as are necessary to keep the copper working easily. The copper works easily when red-hot, but, when cool and continuously hammered, it will crystallize, and it may tear. Therefore during the belling operation anneal the metal often. Keep turning the pipe as it is being belled, and do not strike hard enough to distort the belling. When the pipe is belled sufficiently to make the skirt of the branch, work the copper over, forming the saddle; then anneal the saddle, and, while red-hot, drop it on the pipe that it is to fit, and form it to the pipe with a small wooden mallet. Do not leave sharp shoulders on the branches; besides weakening them, these shoulders make it difficult to match the hole in the pipe to the branch. Trim the branch to about the shape shown in the illustrations. Avoid excessive skirting, since it merely thins the metal at the edge and does not make the branch stronger.

Opening the hole in the pipe is the next operation. Wire the branch onto the pipe and fit it to the spot where it must go.

After the branch has been wired, make scribe markings, as shown in Fig. 24; then remove the branch and lay out for opening the hole. The type of layout for opening the hole differs, depending on the size and shape of the branches. A small branch needs

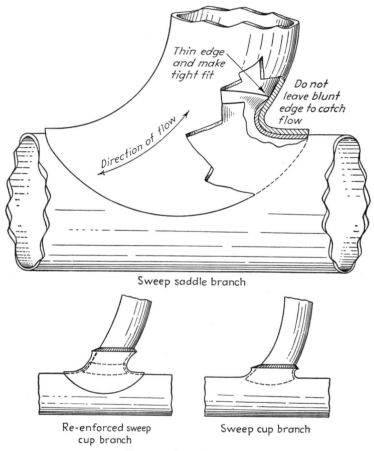

Sweep saddle branch

Re-enforced sweep
cup branch

Sweep cup branch

Fig. 21.—Sweep branches.

only a small round hole at the center of the branch opening, but larger sizes need more of a diamond shape. After making a few branches, the coppersmith will easily learn the proper opening of the branch hole.

**Sweep Branches.**—The saddle branch is also made on a "sweep." This type of branch greatly aids the direction of flow and reduces friction in pipe systems. It is made by bending the pipe first, then working the saddle in or near the bend itself. Figure 21 shows sweep branches, the saddle sweep, the cup with reinforcing collar, and the cup branch with a sweep.

The sweep, if made on a saddle branch and made short, can accommodate flow in either direction. The raised collar inside the branch can be thin-edged and smoothed against the sides, to leave no rough edges.

The sweep branch is made by making the required bend for sweep in the pipe before working the branch. The sweep branch has the advantage of coming into the main at right angles and still sweeping into the flow, whereas an angle branch comes directly from an angle. Many times when lines aboard ship are being installed, interference necessitates the use of the sweep branch.

**General Information on Saddle Branches.**—When making a saddle branch, use material of slightly heavier gauge than that of the pipe that it is to fit. The metal at the saddle thins out to some degree from being worked, and, if thin metal is used, the saddle is weakened and the brazing is difficult because of the difference in thickness of the metals.

**Cup Branches with Reinforcing Collar.**—A reinforcing collar is merely a collar fitted and brazed over the top of a cup branch. · The cup branch is first fitted and then brazed. After brazing, the shoulder or lip is trimmed off. The reinforcing collar is then made. It resembles a saddle branch and is fitted and brazed completely through the collar in somewhat the same method as that used in brazing a saddle branch. The reinforcing collar is used also to repair cup branches that have developed leaks during service.

The cup branch is supposed to be the stronger, but it is not used much owing to the difficulty in fabricating.

**Branch Brazing Setup.**—Figure 22 shows a brazing setup for brazing saddle branches with spelter. The coppersmith should closely study each detail and follow every point when setting up and brazing. The setup shown is a typical brazing setup that is still practical, especially when acetylene heat and silver solder are not available. The idea is to arrange the setup to act as an oven so that, when heat is applied, it will be concentrated at the branch.

A large kerosene or gas torch is sufficient for this type of braze. The setup is made so that there is a full circulation of heat completely around the pipe and branch. The coke or bricks should not touch the copper anywhere near the branch,

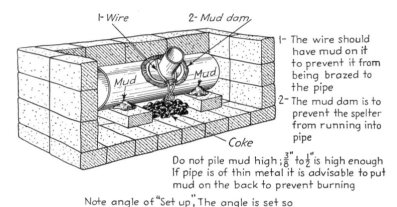

1- Wire        2- Mud dam

1- The wire should have mud on it to prevent it from being brazed to the pipe

2- The mud dam is to prevent the spelter from running into pipe

Do not pile mud high ; $\frac{3}{8}$" to $\frac{1}{2}$" is high enough. If pipe is of thin metal it is advisable to put mud on the back to prevent burning

Note angle of "Set up", The angle is set so that spelter has an easy down hill flow

Wood to keep heat in

About two inches clearance between pipe and brick

Allow two inches clearance between coke and pipe

Inside of pipe is filled with wood

Do not allow coke to touch pipe

Fig. 22.—Spelter brazing a saddle branch.

because the heat generated during brazing would be intensified at the points where the coke or bricks were touching the metal, possibly burning a hole in the copper. For safe brazing practice a **2 in.** clearance is the least to be allowed between the copper and the firebricks or coke.

When setting up the job, a workman can eliminate the possibility of burning the pipe by placing a coating of fire clay on the back of the pipe between the bricks and pipe, where the heat is greatly intensified during the brazing operation. This will protect the pipe, especially if it is made of thin metal.

The branch should be wired on and a tinker's dam placed on the pipe, leaving at least a ½-in. wide trough. This dam is made solely to control the flow of the spelter. Place a ring of fire clay on all pipe edges to protect them from heat; the edges are weak points and are easily burned during brazing. The wires holding the branch on should be coated with fire clay. If the wires become stuck during the brazing process, care should be taken so that a hole is not gouged into the pipe when they are removed. If the wires are stuck on tightly by the spelter, the braze should be heated to a bright cherry red (not to brazing heat) before their removal.

Fill the pipe with wood, placing the wood at the top to form an oven to keep the heat in and to distribute it at the top, back, and bottom of the braze. Apply the spelter with a long-handled spoon, and sprinkle the borax on by hand.

When heating, adjust the torch to a soft-blue flame. Heat the complete section of pipe in the oven, keeping the flame moving, and watch the color of both the pipe and branch. Keep the heat applied so that the complete branch and pipe are of the same color during brazing. Never allow one section to be overheated and another underheated, as this will either burn the metal or make a cold porous braze.

When the same job is prepared for brazing with silver solder or brazing rod, using acetylene heat, the preparation is simplified considerably. The fire clay is not needed; nor is the complicated spelter-brazing setup. The brazing may be done entirely with heat furnished by the acetylene torch, with wood used for backing. The preheating on large sizes may be done with a kerosene torch.

**Inside-brazed Cup Branches.**—Brazing a cup branch from the inside is a slightly different procedure from brazing it from the outside, but the finished job, if done properly, is smooth inside as well as outside.

The method is to work out a hole similar to that of an outside-brazed cup, except the lip, which is intended for spelter braze outside. Bell the branch to fit the inside of the hole. Thin-edge it and clean it. Clean the pipe, insert the branch, and then shape the branch so that the thinned edge is raised slightly while the rest of it fits snugly. Pour borax water through, flushing the parts to be brazed. Place a weight on the branch, as shown in Fig. 23, to keep the branch snug while brazing. Lay borax and spelter on the inside in such a way that when it melts it has a downhill flow into the collar.

When brazing, use two torches, one outside and one inside. The outside torch should be a large kerosene or gas torch, while the inside torch may be either acetylene, hydrogen, or a small gas torch. The outside torch should preheat the complete braze to a medium-red heat before the small torch is brought into use inside. Inside, apply the heat directly on the spelter. Make sure that the spelter completely fills the collar at the outside; if the spelter is not showing entirely around the outside, add more spelter and melt it. When it finally shows at the outside, place more spelter and borax in the pipe, and then keep the heat concentrated at the point inside where the spelter lies. When the spelter melts, bump the copper smoothly down inside the pipe with a steel ball. **Wear goggles while doing this.** After the pipe is cleaned and surplus spelter is ground away, the job should be smooth, both inside and outside.

**Marking or Scribing Flanges and Branches.**—Before the common use of the acetylene torch and silver solder, nearly all flanges and branches marked on the job for shop fabrication were scribed with a compass, a mark being scratched into the metal. These marks were made while the pipe was being fitted into its place and prepared for shop fabrication. Branches were wired on and then marked. The flanges, held in place by turning the copper slightly over the face of the flange, were bolted together and then marked. When being prepared for brazing, the flanges and branches were fitted to these marks.

Since the introduction of acetylene and silver solder, many changes have affected various coppersmithing operations, and one is the marking of branches and flanges. Branches are now tacked on by means of silver solder and an acetylene torch instead of by wiring and scribing. The scribing is done just before the branch is removed from the pipe to open the hole, as shown in Fig. 24. Most silver-brazing flanges are now fitted and brazed on the job.  Only the larger sizes are tacked in place and then removed to the shop for completion because of both the great heat necessary and the danger of fire.

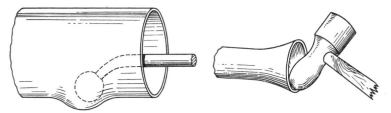

Bump out Cup in Usual Manner        Shape Branch to Fit Cup

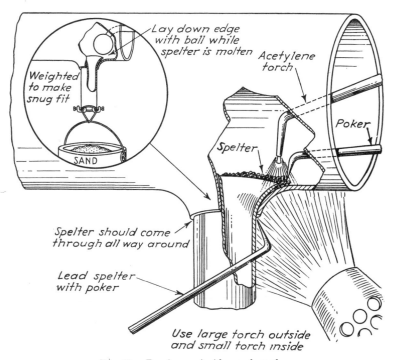

Fig. 23.—Brazing an inside cup branch.

When marking flanges, especially large flanges (4 in. and up), to be spelter brazed, one should never place fewer than three scribe marks at equal distances apart.  The same rule may be followed when marking branches.  When scribing a large branch, center punch it, usually in four or more places equidistant apart. Place one point of the compass into the center-punch hole, and

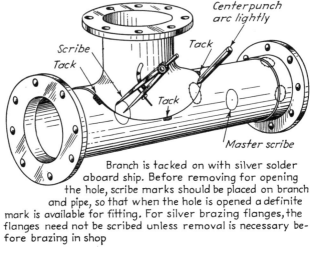

Branch is tacked on with silver solder aboard ship. Before removing for opening the hole, scribe marks should be placed on branch and pipe, so that when the hole is opened a definite mark is available for fitting. For silver brazing flanges, the flanges need not be scribed unless removal is necessary before brazing in shop

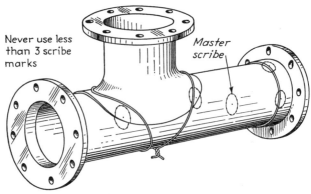

This branch has been wired on, instead of being tacked with silver solder.
Scribe flange while in place aboard ship. Flanges are also scribed in place or tacked with silver solder aboard ship

Fig. 24.—Marking flanges and branches.

then swing an arc onto both the branch and the pipe. With a compass make a master scribe in a conspicuous place on the pipe. Make all markings to one scribe setting. This master scribe mark is made for the purpose of checking compass points. Before removing the tacked branch in order to work the branch hole, it is advisable to prick-punch the complete arc made by the compass. This mark will not be easily obliterated by heat or hammering.

**Silver-brazing Branches.**—Brazing branches with silver is becoming preferred to spelter brazing because of the quicker setup, less heat, and no mudding. The larger sizes should be preheated with a large kerosene or gas torch and then finished either with acetylene or with the large torch. The danger of burning is lessened and cleaning is much simpler when the brazing is done with silver solder.

The silver can be so controlled that no filing or grinding is necessary on the finished product. This speed-up of work and the simplicity of accomplishing formerly difficult jobs are very helpful to coppersmiths.

**Branches Made by the Die Method.**—Dies have been developed that enable the coppersmith to make small-diameter branches in copper and copper-nickel lines. The method is similar to the one used in making bell joints. The shape of the die suits the branch contour, and the flaring is done with a specially formed tool that matches the same contour. A special die is used to hold the pipe steady when the hole for the branch is being opened in the pipe. This method is quick and efficient on small piping. On repair work, the branches may be silver brazed while the pipe is in place.

**Plugging a Pipe while Brazing a Branch.**—When a branch is being brazed, the pipe will be difficult to heat if it is not plugged, owing to the cold draft created when heat is applied. It is advisable, therefore, to plug openings, especially if the pipe has a bend that is either hanging downward or is raised. This position creates a natural chimney draft. Cover the ends with a piece of sheet metal or any suitable material.

# CHAPTER X

## TUBE BENDING

There is so much to the tube-bending phase of coppersmithing that it could almost be called a trade by itself. The numerous methods and theories about tube bending sometimes complicate situations that are, in themselves, quite simple. The following chapter is an effort to simplify some of the problems that a coppersmith must be prepared to meet before he starts a job.

The various kinds of bending equipment available are not necessarily essential to coppersmithing unless mass production is practiced. In shipbuilding, however, there is not much mass production, especially on very large ships. Each pipe, then, is an individual problem and must be templated and bent specially to the template. Very few pipes are bent in duplicate, and so it may easily be seen that duplicating machinery is not so essential as individual skill.

Most tubes, if bent empty, that is, without filling of any kind, will flatten out at the section being bent. To prevent this, sand, rosin, lead, or special bending alloy is used as filling to keep the tube from flattening. However, small tubes up to $\frac{1}{2}$ in. I.P.S., especially if they have a wall thickness of more than 0.065 in., can be bent successfully, without filling, on large radius bends merely by heating the section to be bent to an annealing temperature and bending while hot. All other pipes require a filling, and, of the fillings mentioned, sand and rosin are most commonly used.

Sand filling is the quickest and easiest to use, but it can be employed only for large-radius bends and is limited to the smaller piping up to $1\frac{1}{2}$ in. I.P.S. on thin wall or up to 5 or 6 in. on the very heavy wall piping.

Rosin filling can be used in any pipe for any radius bend, no matter how sharp, but, because of the time required for melting the rosin, annealing the pipe, and letting the rosin cool again, it is used only in large-diameter pipes or wherever it is not practical to use sand.

**Sand Filling.**—Dry sand must be used. If sand is wet, it should be dried before using. Drying may be done on a steel plate that is set up on a forge. The plate must be kept red-hot while the sand is shoveled onto it. The sand should be stirred or mixed while heating.

For good results sand should be screened through about ⅛-in. mesh. **If wet sand is used, heating the pipe may cause an explosion. Never use wet or damp sand.**

**Filling a Pipe with Sand.**—Wooden or steel plugs are used to stop the ends of the tube to prevent the sand from pouring out and to keep the sand packed tightly during bending. Steel plugs are used if bending is to be done near the plug, where there is danger of the wooden plug's burning while the pipe is being heated.

Drive a wooden or steel plug into one end of the tube, and then stand the tube on end and fill it with dry sand. Pack the sand solidly by tapping the tube with a wooden mallet or wooden blocks. Keep putting sand into the pipe, and keep tapping the pipe vigorously until the sand level remains full; then plug the top end of the pipe.

Use hard-rolled copper pipe for sand bending. Annealed pipe is easily dented while being filled, and it does not bend well. It has a tendency to bend outside the section being heated.

**Bending.**—If sharp-radius bends are to be made on one end of the pipe, use the end opposite the filling end. The pipe may be set in a vise or on a bending slab, depending on the size of the pipe and the type of bend to be made. The template, or pattern, should then be laid on the pipe to determine where the bends are to be made. Mark the section to be bent by rolling the template on the pipe.

The heat is then applied only to the section of the pipe to be bent (see Fig. 25). Heating is done on small pipes with an acetylene or small gas or kerosene torch. On large piping it is done usually with large kerosene or gas torches.

Heat the pipe until it is completely red on both sides before you bend it. Take care to see that the pipe bends only at the places needed to fit the template. Keep checking with your template to make sure that the bend is being made correctly. If the bend is overbent in some sections, it should be heated at the throat and pulled back while hot. Color knowledge of heat is useful when bending with heat, because copper pipes are easily melted by keeping the heat too long at one spot.

**Repacking Sand.**—When multiple or sharp radius bends are made in pipes, the sand filling may become loose because of the stretch caused while bending, thus flattening the pipe. Some-

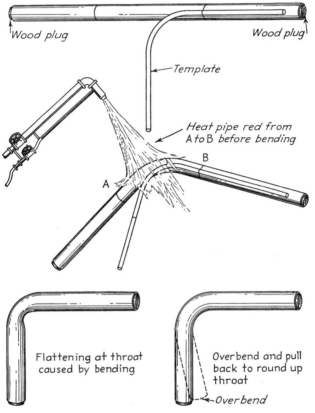

Fig. 25.—Sand bending.

times it is necessary to stand the pipe on end again to repack the sand solidly before completing the other bends. It is advisable to remove the top plug when repacking and to add more sand; otherwise the plug may have to be driven deeply into the pipe.

**Wrinkles in Sand Bending.**—When making sharp bends in sand-filled pipe, it is sometimes difficult to prevent wrinkles from forming at the throat. If they are not allowed to become too deep or too sharp, these wrinkles can be easily prevented by hammering them gently with a round-nosed mallet or planishing hammer as soon as they begin to show. Never allow wrinkles to become deep before hammering them down. As soon as they begin to appear, take care of them.

**Overbending** (see Fig. 25).—When bends are being made in sand-filled pipes, the pipe is often flattened at the throat, a natural condition caused by stretching the pipe on the back of the bend. This is remedied by overbending, *i.e.*, by bending the pipe beyond what is needed to fit the template and then pulling it back to the template. This method rounds the pipe unless the overbend is too great.

Too great an overbend, when pulled back to the template wire, will flatten the pipe at the sides, and so about a 10 per cent overbend is recommended as the proper amount. However, this does not always hold true because situations differ according to how much the pipe is flattened.

**Removing Sand.**—To remove the sand from the pipe after it is bent, the plugs must be removed or the pipe sawed off behind the plug. The plugs in the sand-filled pipe may be removed either by heating the pipe on the end and burning the wood out, by drilling with a brace and bit, or by using a plug puller made of a square file bent over to a 90-deg. angle and sharpened to a flat chisel point on the end.

**Bending Rolls.**—Bending rolls and mechanical equipment are used extensively in the bending of copper and copper-nickel tubing. They are most useful where mass production or duplication of the same bend is required. However, the small portable bending rolls may be used to advantage on many jobs.

Some small tubes of ½ in. O.D. and smaller are in a semi-annealed condition when received by the coppersmith. They can be bent with small hand-bending rolls that can easily be made or purchased from bending-equipment manufacturers. By means of this equipment, bends can be made and the pipe installed without using heat or sand filling. Of course, with mechanical bending equipment, the tubing must be annealed or semiannealed previously. Many easy bends can be made on small tubes by bending with the hands or over the knee. Another method is to slip coil springs over the tube and to bend the tube under the coil spring. This method usually prevents the pipe from flattening, but the spring requires too much time to put on

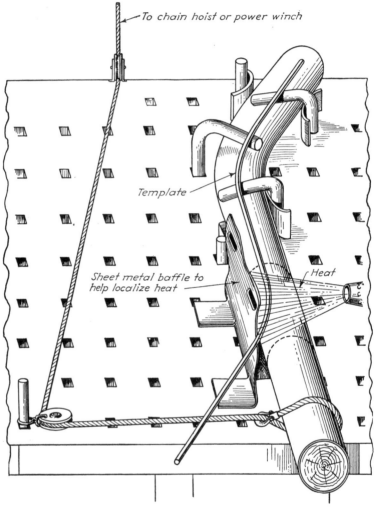

Before attempting to bend a section of pipe, heat that entire portion to a cherry red

FIG. 26.—Sand-bending-slab setup.

and take off. A piece of lead solder in the wire form, wrapped tightly around a small tube and the tube bent by hand, can also be used to advantage when other facilities are not available.

**Sand-bending Slab Setup** (see Fig. 26).—Heavy-walled pipes of larger diameters may be bent hot when sand filled. The slab setup is typical of hot bending operations, and the various points should be closely observed:

Fill the pipe with sand and tamp it to pack the sand tightly. When tamped, plug it, lay it on the slab, and then secure it solidly with dogs and pins. Do not place pins too close to the section that is to be bent; it may crush the hot pipe when bending pressure is exerted against it. If the pipe rests directly on the slab, it will be difficult to heat. If possible, always place a small pipe underneath the pipe being bent to keep it from resting directly on the steel slab.

Arrange the steel cable and pulley so that it will be pulling at right angles to the pipe. A power winch is very handy in this case, but a chain hoist may be used to serve the same purpose. The baffle plate behind the section being heated serves to keep the heat localized at the section being bent. It may easily be moved whenever necessary.

The section of the pipe to be heated is measured by laying the template on the pipe and then rolling it. Mark the pipe at the points where the template starts to bend. This will give the distance to be heated. The pipe will bend at the section that is heated and should be checked at intervals for proper bend. Watch the progress of the bend closely and apply the heat wherever bending is needed.

The theory of heat application is a point on which many mechanics differ; some say to concentrate the heat at the back of the bend, but some say to apply it to the throat. However, if the pipe were heated so that only the back were red-hot while bending, the back would stretch excessively or break, or it would make a weak point in the pipe. Heating the throat excessively will cause puckering at the throat, a good point, provided that the puckers are not too large to be hammered smooth. The idea is to heat the complete circumference, allowing the pucker at the throat with a minimum stretch at the back.

**Rosin Bending.**—Rosin is a valuable aid to coppersmiths. Its qualities are ideal for use in bending large-diameter and thin-wall pipes on short-radius bends. Rosin is usually brought to the melting stage by the use of steam coils in a vat, or it can be melted on a forge with wood banked high on the sides of a pot or by the use of a torch. A soft flame is used.

Care must be taken to prevent an explosion while using the forge or a torch to melt a pot of rosin. The sides of the container should be heated first, because, if too much heat is applied to the bottom without heating the sides, an explosion will occur.

Copper pipe comes to the coppersmith hard-rolled, and so before it is filled with rosin it must be annealed. It is then left to cool by itself. (No water or acid is used.) When the metal is cool enough so that a wooden plug touching it will not burn, drive the plug in one end, stand the pipe on end, and fill it with molten rosin. The pipe should still be slightly warm when being filled. If it is cold, the rosin will congeal when poured into the pipe, the air pockets will be formed, which make it impossible to work bends without the pipe's caving in. When filled to the top, it is left to cool. A 6-in. pipe usually cools overnight. When cooled, there will be a cone-shaped hole in the rosin at the top end of the pipe due to contraction caused by cooling. If the hole is very deep, pour in more molten rosin; if not very deep, fill with loose (or cold) rosin, drive in the plug, and then the pipe is ready for bending.

**Bending.**—Bending is done either on a bending press or on an anglesmith's slab with a jack. The bending press is undoubtedly better because the pressure required for bending large-diameter piping is very great, and good equipment, of course, is the best insurance for good work.

The pipe is now ready for bending and may be placed on the press. The placing of pegs and blocks or dies is determined by the radius of the bend; here again practice is the best teacher, because the numerous problems that arise must be dealt with individually.

Bending the pipe will cause it to wrinkle or pucker in the throat. This is done purposely to prevent too great stretching on the back of the bend. The puckers must be watched carefully so that they do not become too deep, because deep wrinkles are difficult to hammer out. The general idea is to place as many puckers as the radius will allow, making them small and keeping them well rounded and evenly spaced. If it appears that the radius is too short and puckers would necessarily be too deep for hammering, the pipe should be rough hammered, reannealed, refilled, and rebent. On some extremely sharp radii, a coppersmith may refill a pipe several times before it is finished.

**Hammering Wrinkles or Puckers.**—The pipe to be hammered is laid on a slab. It is good practice to examine both plugs to see that they are not loose, clinching the copper over the plugs thoroughly so that during the hammering the powdered rosin will not escape. In hammering the pipe, the first hammer used is the spanking hammer, or flatter. Bending the pipe will cause it to be slightly oval-shaped at the bend, the sides being raised.

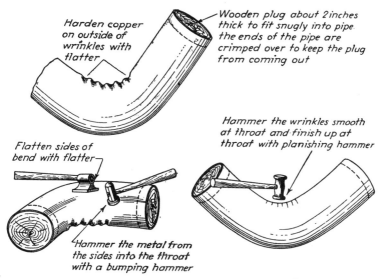

Fig. 27.—Hammering wrinkles from rosin bends.

Using the flatter (see Fig. 27), hammer down the sides at the bend a little below round, making the pipe oval the opposite way. Then use a bumping hammer and start hammering at the sides of the pipe, hammering the wrinkles toward the center of the throat. Turn the pipe from side to side until a $V$ is shaped at the throat. When the throat is hammered and the pipe is nearly round, it should be planished and dressed down. If slight rebending is necessary, it should be done before planishing. The plugs are removed when the hammering is completed, and the next step is to melt out the rosin.

**Melting the Rosin.**—Raise the pipe on a chain hoist until it has a good downhill fall for melting out the rosin. Using a torch with a soft flame, apply the heat first to the bottom of the pipe until the rosin flows out; then gradually raise the torch until the rosin is all removed.   Then anneal the pipe and clean it in a sulphuric acid bath to make it ready for fitting.

**Safety.**—Wear goggles and gloves while handling molten rosin. Always start melting rosin at the *bottom*.

*Never* apply heat to rosin-filled pipe; always bend it cold.

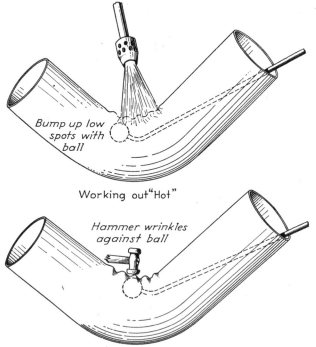

Bump up low
spots with
ball

Working out "Hot"

Hammer wrinkles
against ball

The same care must be taken in working
wrinkles hot as when working cold, otherwise the wrinkles may double over and
cause the copper to break

Fig. 28.—Bumping wrinkles.

Rosin is expensive; don't waste or burn it.

Use a soft heat when melting out rosin.

**Characteristics of Hammered Rosin.**—Rosin, when powdered, expands and displaces much more than a solid piece.   This is the principle upon which rosin hammering is based.   When wrinkles are hammered, the rosin underneath expands and becomes a solid backing.   It acts similarly to a dolly or a hammering head, making a solid backing for hammering.   If rosin bends are hammered excessively, it is possible to break the pipe itself because of the powdering and expanding effect.

**Putting out Rosin Fires.**—Often, when rosin is being melted, it will catch fire. The best method of extinguishing rosin fires is by smothering them. The rosin fires are usually started when the

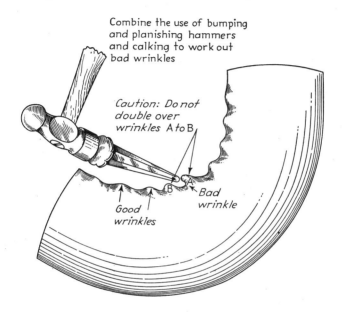

Combine the use of bumping and planishing hammers and calking to work out bad wrinkles

*Caution: Do not double over wrinkles A to B*

B

*Bad wrinkle*

*Good wrinkles*

First hammer with bumping hammer. Examine wrinkle after each few blows. If wrinkle develops a sharp edge or starts doubling over, it should be driven back by using calking tool and ball peen hammer

Fig. 29.—Working out wrinkles by the use of calking tools.

rosin is being melted out of the pipe; the rosin burns in the pot. Put the fire out by placing the lid on the pot, thus smothering it. **Never apply heat to the middle of a pipe that is filled with rosin. Always remove both plugs before melting the rosin from a pipe, beginning at the lower end.**

**Hammering Wrinkles Hot.**—In some cases, when wrinkles are to be hammered, it is quicker to remove the rosin and use a ball and hammer while the pipe is heated. This is done usually on large-diameter pipes when the bends are close to the end of the pipes (see Fig. 28).

**The Use of Calking Tools in Removing Sharp Wrinkles.**—In bending pipe that is rosin filled, it sometimes happens that the wrinkles may be sharp and difficult to remove with hammers alone. In this case, to prevent doubling over the metal and causing breaks, it is advisable to use calking tools in addition to the regular hammers.

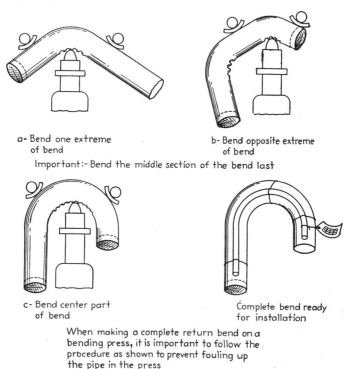

a- Bend one extreme
of bend

b- Bend opposite extreme
of bend

Important:- Bend the middle section of the bend last

c- Bend center part
of bend

Complete bend ready
for installation

When making a complete return bend on a
bending press, it is important to follow the
procedure as shown to prevent fouling up
the pipe in the press

Fig. 30.—Making a return bend on a press (rosin-filled pipe).

When a wrinkle gets to the point shown in Fig. 29, it will be a problem to hammer it down smoothly without causing it to lap over. The pipe should first be hammered as explained in Hammering Wrinkles or Puckers, page 97; then, as the bad wrinkles are hammered, they should be watched carefully so that the wrinkles do not double over. When they show the slightest tendency to lap over, they should be carefully set back with calking tools. This operation may have to be repeated several times before the wrinkle is finally hammered to a smooth-finished job. The slightest lap or crease, if hammered, may cause a leak in the finished job.

**Making a Return Bend on the Bending Press.**—On the bending press, rosin-filled pipes may be bent into various shapes, some of which are quite difficult to make (see Fig. 30). One difficult type of bend is the complete return bend, or the 180-deg. bend. This bend, if not started properly, will get fouled in the press before the bend is completed, making it impossible to finish it in the press.

The proper procedure, then, must be followed to ensure success and to avoid a common type of mistake in making the return bend. Proceed as follows: Roll the template on the pipe, marking the length of the pipe where the bend is to be made. Divide the measured bending length into three equal sections. Bend the two outward sections first; when a sufficient bend is made on the two outward sections, bend the middle section, completing the bend. When bending sand-filled pipe with heat, this precaution is not necessary because the bending press is not used, thus eliminating danger of fouling.

**Bending Coils.**—Making coils of copper or copper-nickel alloy is part of the coppersmith's trade. The coil-bending machine, shown in Fig. 31, while very handy, is not completely essential to the manufacture of coils. Pieces of steel pipe or drums that are of the correct diameter may be used as the forms around which to bend coils.

Figure 31*B* shows a drum setup that is typical of those used by coppersmiths in the bending of coils. Figure 31*A* shows the coil-bending machine. A clamp device (close-up on the sketch) secures the pipe to the proper-sized drum. Heat is then applied to the pipe until it is about cherry-red; the drum is revolved slowly and kept turning as the rest of the tube becomes hot. The desired spacing of coil rise is kept by first marking the rise on the drum with a piece of chalk.

If long coils are to be made, several sections of tubing may be joined either by a cast coupling, cast flanges, or cup joint. When the cup-joint method of joining is used, it is often advisable to work out the cups while the pipe is straight. Working out the cups when the coils are already bent is difficult.

Copper tubing may be bent hot with sand filling or bent cold with rosin filling. Copper-nickel alloy is usually rosin filled for bending. On copper, quicker results are obtained when sand filling and heat are used because the pipe is ready for bending immediately when filled.

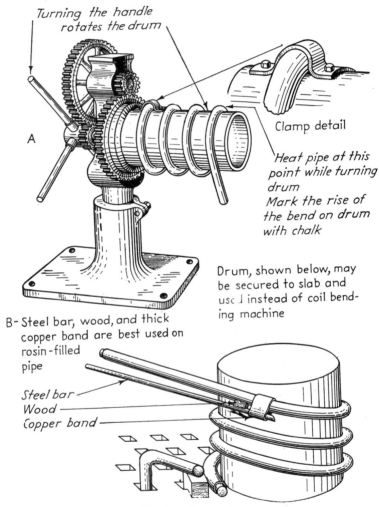

Turning the handle rotates the drum

A

Clamp detail

Heat pipe at this point while turning drum
Mark the rise of the bend on drum with chalk

Drum, shown below, may be secured to slab and used instead of coil bending machine

B- Steel bar, wood, and thick copper band are best used on rosin-filled pipe

Steel bar
Wood
Copper band

FIG. 31.—Coil bending.

Rosin-filled tubing may be bent the same as sand-filled tubing, except that the tube must be annealed before being filled with rosin and then bent cold. Figure 31 shows the bar, wood, and copper-band arrangement for bending rosin-filled coils.

Use steel plugs when sand-filled pipe is bent hot near the end of the pipe, because wooden plugs may burn out, loosening the sand filling and caving or flattening the pipe.

Not all coils are round; they may be rectangular, square, or oval. In this case, the forms are made especially to suit the shape. Before bending a coil, especially if it is a complicated double coil, a template should be made in order to visualize the direction of wind and necessary "kicks." The template can be a miniature made of small-diameter flexible wire; it need not be made to full size.

**Rectangular Tubing.**—A job that often presents difficulties is the templating, bending, and installation of rectangular tubing. This tubing is usually handled by coppersmiths.

There are two main problems regarding this tubing. The first is that of bending. This tubing may be bent as round pipe, but, as it cannot be hammered or worked back into its original shape as can a round pipe, special filling for the tube and special dies are necessary. The second problem is twisting. The tube, being rectangular, occasionally requires a twist in one or both ends besides the regular bends. The twist is necessary because the flange itself cannot be twisted for fitting as it can be in a round tube. The bending and twisting is done while the tube is filled with a bending alloy. It is very important that the pipe be kept from caving or bulging while it is being twisted or bent, because it cannot be reshaped by water pressure or hammering.

**Templating.**—The ship's templates, namely, the wooden template and the center-line template, are made as shown in Fig. 32. The rectangular tube is bent to a center-line template (Fig. 32). When bending the center-line template for rectangular tubing, the mechanic must be careful to allow for the proper side clearance, since the distance will be greater on one side than on the other.

The standard radius of the bends for bending a tube of $1\frac{1}{2}$ by 3 in. is 18 in. This is the rule no matter which way the bend is made, whether through the flat or through the longer section of the rectangle. Convenient bending radii for other sizes should be worked out on the job.

**Annealing.**—Since rectangular tubing is usually brass or bronze, the annealing must be done with care because these metals cannot stand so much heat as copper can. The work should be heated to a dark-red color for annealing, about 1000°F.

Two torches should be used, one on each side of the tube, to prevent it from bowing. Applying the heat to just one side will

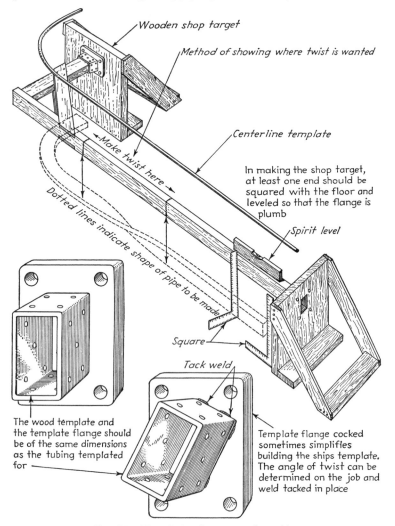

In making the shop target, at least one end should be squared with the floor and leveled so that the flange is plumb

FIG. 32.—Templating for rectangular tubing.

cause the tube to bow. Anneal only the section to be bent or twisted.

**Bending Alloy.**—The filling that gives best satisfaction is a bending alloy composed of bismuth, lead, tin, and cadmium.

This composition is melted by submerging the pot in a vat of boiling water. There should be a valve or spigot in or near the bottom of the pot for convenient pouring.

**Filling.**—After the annealed tube has been allowed to cool, it is set up on an angle near the pot of molten alloy and plugged tightly at the bottom end. The most satisfactory plug is a plate of copper or brass, silver soldered onto the end of the tube.

Apply a coating of oil to the inside of the tube, making sure that it is well applied. If oil or some lubricant is not used, the alloy will have a tendency to cling to the tube walls.

Just before filling the tube with alloy, warm it thoroughly either by steaming it or by pouring hot water on its outside surface or directly into the tube. The tube is then ready for filling. Raise the pot of bending alloy from the boiling water with a chain hoist, open the spigot, and fill.

As soon as the tube is filled to its required level, it should be cooled by applying a stream of cold water to the lowest point and gradually raising the stream toward the upper end. Do not cool from the top down because hollow places or air pockets, due to metal shrinkage, will result and may eventually cause the tube to cave in during the bending operation. The alloy solidifies almost immediately on cooling, leaving the tube ready for bending.

**Bending.**—Bending is done on the same type of press as that used for ordinary rosin bending. The tube is marked for bending in the same manner as is round tubing. It is also placed in a press in the same way. The wood blocks between the bending-press pegs and the tube should be of hardwood and of sufficient strength not to bend or break. If the wood bends or breaks, it will leave a dent in the tube, and on certain types of work where rectangular brass tubing is used the side-wall-variance specifications are very rigid.

This tube, being rectangular, must have at least two dies for bending, one to fit each side of its rectangular shape. These dies must be made to a safe radius for bending the tube. Bending the tube to too sharp a radius results in distorting or wrinkling it.

**Bending Procedure.**—The actual bending is done similarly to the bending of round rosin-filled tubes. The bending section is marked; the die is slipped over the tube; then the press is brought against it gradually, just a small amount being bent at a time, then the die being moved a little. This last procedure is continued until the complete section is partly bent; then the entire process is repeated. Bending in this gradual manner prevents distortion and results in a much smoother bend.

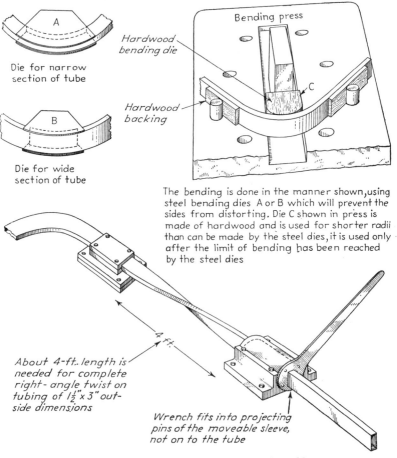

Die for narrow section of tube

Die for wide section of tube

Bending press

Hardwood bending die

Hardwood backing

The bending is done in the manner shown, using steel bending dies A or B which will prevent the sides from distorting. Die C shown in press is made of hardwood and is used for shorter radii than can be made by the steel dies, it is used only after the limit of bending has been reached by the steel dies

About 4-ft. length is needed for complete right-angle twist on tubing of $1\frac{1}{2}"$ x 3" outside dimensions

Wrench fits into projecting pins of the moveable sleeve, not on to the tube

Fig. 33.—Bending and twisting rectangular tubing.

**Twisting.**—The twisting is done by gripping the tube into two snug-fitting dies that are about 8 to 10 in. long (Fig. 33). One is stationary and is solidly secured to an anglesmith's slab; the other, which is also solidly secured, has a movable sleeve that can be twisted with a large wrench, thus twisting the tube. No tools other than the dies are used against the tube in the twisting operation.

A full 4 ft. of length is generally used for a complete right-angle twist to prevent distortion during twisting. The workman should practice twisting rectangular tubing, using short scraps, to ascertain for himself just how much twisting can be done on short lengths.

**Removing the Filling.**—The best means yet devised to remove the filling is a troughlike vat sufficiently deep for a large portion of the tube to be submerged in boiling water. The trough should be on a slight slope and should have a spigot at the lower end to allow removal of the alloy as it flows to the bottom. Steam applied to the outside of tube will not melt the alloy completely; it is best to submerge the tube, allowing it to be heated inside as well as outside.

When the bending alloy is removed, the tube should be cleaned inside with a blast of steam to melt and blow out all remaining particles.

**Fitting.**—The flanges are fitted onto the tube in the shop to targets (shop templates), then silver brazed or sweated on as local specifications indicate. The tube should not be annealed before installation.

**Cleaning.**—Final cleaning is done by warming the tube, then immersing it in an acid bath. All trace of acid should be washed off with water, and the tube should be scrubbed with fine sand, then thoroughly dried.

## CHAPTER XI

## TEMPLATING

"To template" means to make a pattern or a guide, and it may be done by any one of the various ways of taking measurements for facilitating the making of bends in a pipe. The template may be a piece of $\frac{1}{4}$-in. wood carved with a knife to the measurement of a peculiar bend or clearance that may be necessary, or it may be a piece of solid rod or a small piece of tube with which the center-line measurement of a pipe is templated. It may be a wooden template built between two or more pipe openings aboard ship to get the bolthole and face-to-face measurements; it may also be a shop template, which is only a transfer template of the ship's wooden template, built in the shop and sometimes called a "target" in order to distinguish it from the others.

Templates are also made from sheet metal, cardboard, pieces of wire, old condenser tubing, steel pipe, or any available material, depending on what kind of work or situation is involved. When the regular material (rods or pieces of pipe or pine wood) is not available, the mechanic must devise his own makeshifts to take care of the job. The makeshifts, of course, are unlimited, since the ingenuity of the workman is involved.

Almost all pipes are bent before being installed aboard ship. The bending is necessary because of the arrangement of the machinery, etc., aboard ship. Each pipe is bent to an individual shape, which is determined by obstructions encountered and by the position of the pipe openings. Most pipes are templated aboard ship with a rod or a piece of tubing. This template may be of any material that can be easily bent. When they are available, old scrap tubes from condensers are very good for this purpose.

**Center-line Template.**—A center-line template is measured at the center of the pipe fitting or flange, from opening to opening. It shows the exact center line of the pipe it represents and shows all the curves and the bends that the pipe must have when it is finished.

**Discs.**—Sheet-metal or cardboard discs are sometimes used to measure clearances on the sides of the template. The discs are cut to the diameter of the pipe, plus whatever lagging is to be added, and then slipped over the center-line template. Moving the disc along the template will show places of interference that must be corrected by rebending the template. When the discs move through the entire length of the template without touching, and there is no spring or strain where the template enters the spider, the template is ready for removal to the shop.

**Flange Spider** (see Fig. 34).—The flange spider is a device used to facilitate center-line templating. It is bolted onto the face of the flange and then centered. The center opening on the flange spider is just large enough to allow the template rod to enter without much slack. The spider serves as a center and square for the template, allowing the template to enter the opening only when it is accurately bent. If even a slight force is necessary to insert the template in the spider, the template is not true and needs more adjustment.

**Radius.**—Make all radii as large as practicable for ease in bending the pipe. If a radius is made too sharp, there is a risk of breaking the back of the pipe or excessively wrinkling the throat during bending. A safe working rule for bending a template is "Radius of bend = $2\frac{1}{2}$ to 3 times the diameter of the pipe."

**Piece Templates.**—When bends are all on one plane, it is easy to use a template rod while bending; however, when bends have more than one plane, it is impossible to lay a template anywhere on the pipe to get an accurate template reading. This is overcome by making piece templates of the bends from the master template and laying them separately on the different bends.

Care should be taken when templates are bent that there are no unnecessary "kicks," or bends, in the finished template. As many of the bends as possible should be made on one plane. Avoid unnecessarily making two bends in one (a bend on a bend), as this is usually difficult.

**Templating Follow-up, Ship Template** (see Fig. 34).—Wooden templates are used with rod or wire templates in some cases, when

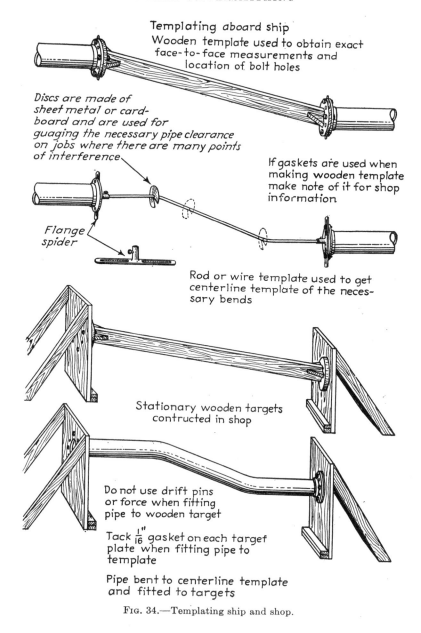

Templating aboard ship

Wooden template used to obtain exact face-to-face measurements and location of bolt holes

Discs are made of sheet metal or cardboard and are used for guaging the necessary pipe clearance on jobs where there are many points of interference.

If gaskets are used when making wooden template make note of it for shop information

Flange spider

Rod or wire template used to get centerline template of the necessary bends

Stationary wooden targets contructed in shop

Do not use drift pins or force when fitting pipe to wooden target

Tack $\frac{1}{16}''$ gasket on each target plate when fitting pipe to template

Pipe bent to centerline template and fitted to targets

Fig. 34.—Templating ship and shop.

sections of pipes are templated aboard ship, because they enable the mechanic to complete the section of pipe from the form in the shop without an extra trip to the ship to fit it. Sometimes the place where the fitting is to be done is so awkward to work in that it is better to do as much work as possible in the shop. Sometimes, too, the job is too large to handle on the spot, as it requires the use of chain falls and large heating equipment.

Figure 34 shows the steps necessary in a templating job. Whenever possible, make templates from a soft wood, such as white pine. The wooden blanks are cut round, to the outside diameter of the flange, drilled, and faced smoothly. They are bolted onto the openings for which the template is to be made. The number of bolts used in tightening the blank onto the flange depends on the size of the flange. A 6-in. I.P.S. flange needs only three or four bolts; larger flanges may need more. The main object is to hold the wooden plates tightly against the flange. If the openings are directly opposite each other, pieces of gasket material or cardboard should be placed between the blanks and the flange; otherwise the template may be difficult to remove from between the flanges after it is finished. A notation should be made for shop information as to whether or not gaskets were used when making the template aboard ship, because gasket allowance is usually added to the template in the shop unless the worker is otherwise instructed.

Join the two wooden blanks with a long piece of board as shown. A snug fit without any strain must be made. Tack the board onto the blanks and then fit the side brackets onto the blank and the board. When they fit perfectly, nail them down, but make sure that the pieces are not forced one way or the other by the hammering. When both ends have been nailed, remove the bolts from one end of the template to check for possible strain. If there is strain, the removal of bolts from either side will show it by springing the template either against the pipe flange or away from it. In case there is strain, the template should be taken apart and refitted.

A rod or wire center-line template should also be taken to get the shape of the pipe bends and also to make possible a check for clearances. Sometimes when there are many clearance points, instead of measuring with a rule a cardboard or metal disc is cut to the outside diameter of the pipe and is slipped onto the template rod and moved from clearance point to clearance point.

The flange spider is bolted onto the face of the flanges, the template rod being inserted into it.   If the template rod binds when it is being inserted, the bind must be removed by rebending. The spider, in this case, serves as a square.

When both the wooden and rod templates are finished, make all necessary notations, such as which end of the rod template corresponds to the wooden template, whether or not an allowance has already been made for gaskets, and also make a mark showing which way the pipe will fit when it is returned to the ship.   Tag the template for pipe size, and note whether the pipe should be tinned and wiped; mark the locations for bosses or branches.

**Shop Template.**—Constructing the target in the shop is the next step.   Read the information tagged to the template, or consult with the mechanic who made the template, to make sure about gasket allowance, etc.   Select knot-free pine about 2 in. thick for target plates and allow about 2 to 3 in. width on the sides.   Whenever possible, set the wooden template on blocks on the floor so that both flange facings are at right angles to the floor.   Then set the plates against the template facings and mark on the plate the flange holes through the blank template flange; also mark the outside of the blanks on the plate.   After marking them, drill the holes and cut a hole out of the center of the flange circle large enough to allow the pipe that is to be fitted to slip through easily.   When the plates are drilled and the center has been cut out, bolt the plates to the template.   Make sure at this point about the gasket allowance.   Then tack the plate to a wooden floor and fit and nail the brackets, securing the plate solidly as shown in Fig. 34.

After the target has been made, bend the pipe to the centerline template and fit it to the target.   When it is bent, slip the pipe into the holes that were made in the plates, mark the pipe for the flange, cut one end off and put one flange on, place pipe back in the template, bolt the flange onto the template, and then mark the other end.   When both ends have been fitted, the flanges may be marked and removed for brazing or tacked onto the pipe with silver solder; then they are removed from the template and the brazing is finished while the pipe is out of the template.

A close fit of the pipe being installed depends on the care taken during each operation, from the ship template to the final marking, tacking, and brazing. Extreme care should be taken so that the templates are not bumped or forced out of shape, even very slightly, while being handled. An error in any one of the several steps will make the finished product a misfit.

# CHAPTER XII
## EXPANSION JOINTS

An expansion joint is a short section of pipe with a bellows formed in it. The bellows may be formed either inward or outward, and it is usually fitted with flanges on both ends. This bellows makes a flexible joint which absorbs the excess vibration that might otherwise break the pipe.

Expansion joints are used to absorb movement caused by the vibration of machinery, the expansion and contraction caused by heating and cooling, the sudden jar caused by firing guns, and the buckling of bulkheads caused by the natural pitching of the ship during a storm. Expansion joints are also used to connect machinery, as in the exhaust line connecting a steam turbine of a generator plant to the auxiliary condenser, or between the main condenser and the sea valves. The purpose of this joint is to allow external expansion. There is a mistaken idea that the expansion joint takes care of fluctuating internal pressures. This is untrue, because if any expansion joint is subjected to too much pressure, it becomes distorted and has to be removed and reworked by the coppersmith in order to return it to the original shape. There are several types of expansion joints made especially for use in different situations. These may be classified into four general classes: the convex, the concave, the expansion loop, and the ogee.

The convex expansion joint is the type most commonly used in marine work; its good feature is that it can be easily manufactured from either tubing or sheet copper and can be made by hand or hydraulically.

The concave type is used where the distance between the valves or machinery is very close, necessitating a very short joint. It is not so efficient as the convex type, but it serves the purpose in absorbing the vibrations and strain between pumps or sections of machinery.

The expansion loop (Fig. 37) is used extensively on small-diameter pipe systems. Small-diameter pipe is not very success-

114

fully worked into the different types of expansion joints, because it is too difficult to make and does not have enough flexibility. The expansion loop is just as efficient in this case.

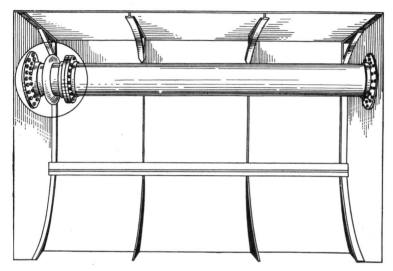

Bellows convex type expansion joint
This type is used when pipe must be straight
or when large diameter pipe is used

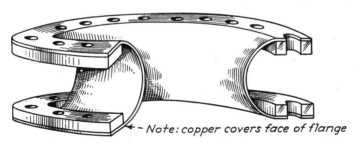

Concave expansion joint
This type is used when the distance between
valves or machinery is too short to allow the
longer convex type

Fig. 35.—Expansion joints.

The ogee-type expansion serves the same purpose as the convex double-bellows type. It is seldom used.

**Expansion Joint, Convex Type.**—Figure 35 illustrates a bellows-type expansion joint in a typical operating installation, showing bulkhead-to-bulkhead hookup. This type of expansion joint is also used when fitting pipe to vibrating machinery. If solid pipe were used in these places, the strain of excessive vibration would be placed on the pipe, flanges, or machinery castings, and often the pipe or castings would break or develop leaks from vibration. This trouble is eliminated by the use of the expansion joint. The flexibility of the expansion joint removes the strain from the fittings and the machinery, and the strain is absorbed by the bellows. Expansion joints should be removed occasionally and annealed, because they become hardened from vibration.

**Convex Type (Made Hydraulically).**—Expansion joints with any number of bellows can be made hydraulically. As many as thirteen bellows have been made on one joint; however, on most work, one or two bellows are enough. Expansion joints can be made of copper, brass, copper-nickel, steel, and bronze, but are usually made of copper, because in service it is more flexible than the other metals.

Special dies and some equipment are necessary. The principle involved in this manufacture is very simple, and most shops that have a hydraulic press for bending pipe can easily make the smaller sizes. The method of manufacture, in brief, is to clamp a pipe into an expansion-joint die which has partitions that may be used if more than one bellows is desired. The die ends have a cupped leather arrangement to hold the pressure internally. These leathers are held in place by end plates, which, in turn, are held together by being squeezed in a press. A high-pressure water pump with about 5,000 lb. per sq. in. capacity is necessary. Either the hand pump or the power-operated pump may be used, but the power-operated pump is more satisfactory, as it gives a steadier pressure. The hand-operated pump gives a fluctuating pressure that is likely suddenly to increase the pressure to the bursting point of the expansion joint if some means of bleed off are not provided.

When the cylinder and expansion die are set up in the press with a snug pressure against both ends, the internal pressure is pumped in until enough pressure is injected to start swelling the bellows. As the bellows start moving outward, the press should be brought together slowly. Coordination of external and internal pressure is absolutely necessary here, because, if too much pressure is added, the joint will burst, and, if the end pres-

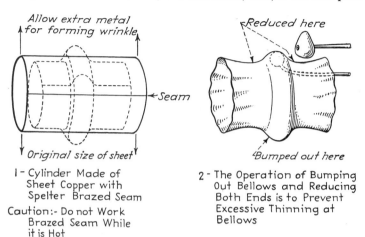

1 – Cylinder Made of Sheet Copper with Spelter Brazed Seam

Caution:- Do not Work Brazed Seam While it is Hot

2 – The Operation of Bumping Out Bellows and Reducing Both Ends is to Prevent Excessive Thinning at Bellows

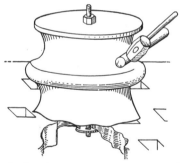

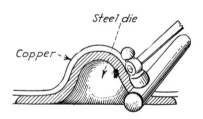

3 – Squeeze the Expansion Joint Together with Large Bolt and Flange. Shape with bar and Hammer as Shown to Form the Expansion Bellows

4 – Use Bar and Hammer To Form Copper Against Hammering Die. Hammering Die for Planishing Made to Suit Job

Fig. 36.—Operations in making an expansion joint.

sure is too fast, the bellows will buckle inward. In either extreme, failure will be the result. The ideal way is to keep the bellows expanding and to keep the ends coming together so that the bellows are flat across the top, not rounded. The actual appearance is the best gauge to use. The allowance for bellows is made by figuring the stretch out of the curve and adding it to the length of the dies.

**Making a Convex Expansion Joint (Hand Method).**—Figure 36 shows the operations in making an expansion joint by the hand method. Lay out the copper for the expansion joint as shown in 1, the diameter of the cylinder being the halfway mark between the bottom and the top of the finished bellows. Make the sheet a few inches long to compensate for the shortening that occurs when the metal is pressed together. Mark the section to be bumped out on the outside with a scratch awl and a prick punch, so that, when the copper is heated, the marks will be visible. Bump with a ball as shown in 2; watch the marks and keep the bumped section even and rounded, not sharp. Always hammer the seam when the copper is cold; do not attempt to stretch or work the seam while it is red-hot, because the spelter becomes brittle when hot, sometimes called "short hot," and may break if worked, making it necessary to patch or re-braze the job.

The next operation is to reduce the cylinder on both sides of the bellows, starting at the bellows and working toward the end, as shown. After both ends have been reduced, anneal the bellows and set the joint on an anglesmith's slab. Bolt the expansion joint as shown in part 3, forcing it together, then hammer. This will aid in shaping the metal at the bellows. When one side is worked, turn the joint over and repeat the same operation on the other side. After both sides have been worked and the bellows is taking the required shape, place it on a hammering die and finish hammering it with a planishing hammer. Any size of expansion joint can be made by hand with this method and simple tools.

**Concave Expansion Joint.**—The concave expansion joint shown in Fig. 35, can be made to fit into narrow and close places. This, of course, is its main feature, because this type is not so efficient as the bellows type. The method of manufacture is similar to the one used for making Van Stone flanges. The copper is first bumped down at the middle, rounding out the concave curve; then the ring flanges are slipped on and the copper is flanged over the complete face of the flanges and drilled through for boltholes. When flanging over the copper, do not make a sharp edge at the curve of the flange. Make the radius as large as may be allowed. A sharp radius creates a weak point that may break from vibration. The ring flanges are made of steel or of flat iron bars bent into a circle, welded together, and drilled.

Note:- This is a Plan View, Bend Must be Level in Steam or Air Lines to Prevent Water Accumulation

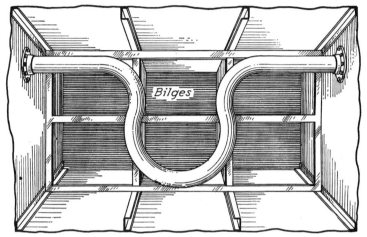

The Expansion Caused by Steam or Movement of Ship's Bulkheads is Compensated for by the Flexibility of this Type of Bend

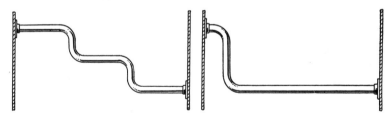

Different Bends which Will Absorb the Vibration and Strain

Fig. 37.—Expansion loops and bends.

**Expansion Bends.**—Figure 37 shows the expansion loop and some bends that will serve the same purpose on lines where expansion and contraction or vibration is excessive. This loop is the most commonly used type of expansion fitting on small lines, and it is easy to make. When using the loop type on steam or air lines, the loop should be horizontal so that the loop does not create a water pocket. The loop is bent in a horse shoe or reentrant curve. The larger the loop, the more flexibility it has.

On board ship when a line runs from bulkhead to bulkhead, it is not always necessary to use the expansion loop. Ordinary bends, such as those shown, usually are sufficient to take care of the expansion, contraction, and vibration that may occur.

On high-pressure steam lines the loop type of expansion joint is used almost entirely (plus bends wherever it is possible to put

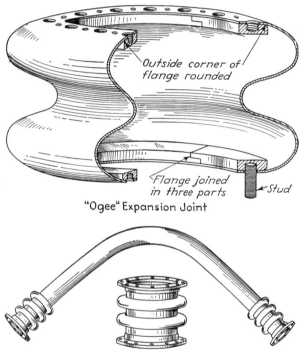

*Outside corner of flange rounded*

*Flange joined in three parts* *Stud*

"Ogee" Expansion Joint

Multiple Type Expansion Joints Made by the Hydraulic Method

Fig. 38.—Expansion joints.

them), because it is a very efficient compensation for the great amount of expansion and contraction caused by heating and cooling. For small tubing a complete loop, or "pigtail," is used.

**Ogee Type of Expansion Joint.**—The ogee-type expansion joint (Fig. 38) is made of sheet copper. A three-piece split-ring steel flange is used on this type because it is inserted after the expansion is made.

The manufacture of this expansion joint is in many ways similar to the manufacture of the external bellows type (hand made). The original size of the cylinder before the joint is made is equal to the diameter halfway between the inner and outer curves, not at the extreme outside diameter and not at the extreme inside diameter. This gives the finished product a more even thickness, as was mentioned in the bellows type of expansion joint. Bumping the copper out at the ends forms the convex curve, and reducing the center forms the concave. When the curves are formed and planished to fit the template layout, determine the length, and work the ends over to form the flat flange surface.

Place the expansion joint in a wooden target and mark the holes for drilling. When drilled, place the split flanges inside the expansion joint and screw on with flat-headed screws countersunk into the face of the copper flange and tapped into the steel' to hold the steel flanges intact. Face the flanges smoothly with a file, removing all burns and protrusions. Anneal all types of expansion fittings before installing them.

# CHAPTER XIII

## SHEET BRAZING

The most satisfactory way to join copper sheets is by brazing them together with spelter. The reason is that the seam can be made smooth, as strong as the sheet itself, ductile, and almost imperceptible.

Sheets may be brazed together to make cylinders, pipes, and many other special fittings. Small sheets may be brazed together to make a larger sheet, which then may be used instead of a large new sheet. Very thin copper sheets and heavy-gauge sheets can be brazed with equally good results. Before being brazed, the sheets are thin-edged, lapped to the depth of the thinned edge, fluxed with borax, and then brazed over a forge or with a torch.

Thin-gauge small work can easily be held with tongs during the brazing process, but heavy-gauge large work is usually suspended with a chain hoist or other convenient equipment.

**Layout Allowance.**—When a cylinder is made from sheet copper, the seam to be spelter brazed, allowance must be made for the seam and for metal thickness. This allowance depends on the thickness of the sheet. The formula for sheet layout is based on either the inside or the outside measurements; for example, a sheet $\frac{1}{4}$ in. thick is to be rolled into a cylinder 8 in. in diameter. Multiply $8 \times 3.1416$, which equals approximately $25\frac{1}{8}$ in. This, then, equals the neutral diameter, not the inside or the outside diameters. The neutral diameter is the exact center of the thickness of the sheet, measured diametrically when the sheet is rolled. To get an inside diameter measurement, add three times the thickness of the sheet to the neutral diameter, or, in this case, $3 \times \frac{1}{4}$ in., which will be

$$\frac{3}{4} + 25\frac{1}{8} = 25\frac{7}{8} \text{ in.}$$

To get the outside measurement, subtract three times the thickness, or $25\frac{1}{8} - \frac{3}{4} = 24\frac{3}{8}$ in. The next step is to add the seam allowance.

The chart in Fig. 39 shows that the lap of the seam for ¼-in. copper is 1¼ in.  One half of 1¼ = ⅝ in.; this, then, would be added to the neutral diameter, 25⅛ plus or minus ¾ + ⅝ in.

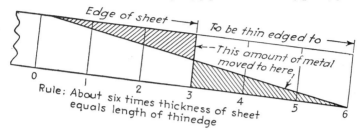

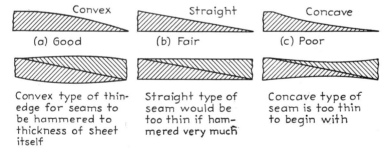

THINEDGING CHART

| Sheet decimals | Fractions | Length of thinedge |
|---|---|---|
| .032 | 1/32 " | 1/4 " |
| .062 | 1/16 " | 1/2 " |
| .125 | 1/8 " | 3/4 " |
| .1875 | 3/16 " | 1 1/8 " |
| .25 | 1/4 " | 1 3/16 " |
| .3125 | 5/16 " | 1 1/4 " |
| .375 | 3/8 " | 1 1/4 " |

On heavy metal the limit for seam lap is about 1¼"

Examples of possible seam combinations

| Convex | Straight | Concave |
|---|---|---|
| (a) Good | (b) Fair | (c) Poor |

Convex type of thin-edge for seams to be hammered to thickness of sheet itself

Straight type of seam would be too thin if hammered very much

Concave type of seam is too thin to begin with

FIG. 39.—The thin-edge lap seam.

An error of ½ in. in the length of a sheet for a 30-in. diameter would not apparently make any noticeable difference in the diameter, but an error of ½ in. on the length of a sheet for a 6-in. diameter would obviously show considerably.  Actually, the increase in diameter is the same in both large and small diameters. Therefore, in the laying out for smaller diameters, especially on heavy-gauge material, accuracy is very important.

**Thin Edging.**—Sheets are thin-edged by being laid upon an anvil and having the edge hammered to a taper so that, when the two tapered edges are together, a smooth seam results. Heavy copper is thin-edged with a medium-weight cross-peen hammer, and thin-gauge copper may be thin-edged with any ordinary hammer that has a suitably flat facing. A general rule for thin edging is six times the thickness of the metal equals the length of the thin edge (see Fig. 39).

After the sheets have been thin-edged, they should be annealed and cleaned. A sheet, when thin-edged, has a tendency to bow slightly. This bow should be removed and the thinned edge should be straight and free of ragged edges before it is laid up to be brazed.

Sometimes clamps, also called "dovetails" or "cramps," are cut into copper seams before the brazing in order to hold the seam together tightly during the brazing. These clamps are cut at intervals along the thin edge with a chisel so that the clamps or dovetails all lift on one side. They must be cut on an angle to make a good fit. Clamps are not used very much in modern shops, because they weaken the seam, and, when the seam is worked or hammered, breaks or tears usually develop at the bottom of the chisel cut, resulting in leaks.

**Theory of Thin-edge Lap** (see Fig. 39).—*a*, *b*, and *c* show three ways of thin edging a sheet for brazing. *a* shows that the convex thin edge, when brazed together, results in a thick rounded seam. This seam is best when a smooth-hammered finished product is desired. Hammering the seam after it has been brazed will bring the thickness of the seam itself to the thickness of the sheet and at the same time make a smooth-appearing job. *b* shows a straight-tapered thin edge, which is most commonly used, particularly on jobs where no hammering is done afterward. When hammered, the straight-tapered thin edge becomes thinner than the sheet, and a weakness results, but on sheets where hammering is not necessary it makes a neat seam. *c* shows a poor seam thin edge, which is not recommended. The thickness of the seam after the brazing is less than the thickness of the copper. This thin edge is produced only by inexperienced mechanics.

**Cleaning before Thin Edging.**—Before thin edging copper sheets, especially on heavy-gauge material, the coppersmith should anneal the sheet edges and remove all dirt or oxide by either scraping or wire brushing the sheet. The slab or anvil that is to serve as backing during the thin-edging operation should be free of dirt and reasonably smooth. If dirty copper is thin edged or if dirty equipment is used in thin edging, the

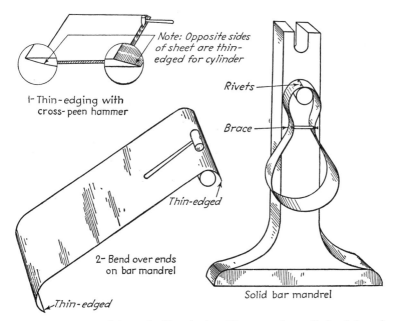

Fig. 40.—Thin-edging and rolling sheets. The copper is so rolled and shaped that a tension holds it together at the seam before rivets are placed. When one rivet is set the waves and slack should be taken out of both seams before second rivet is drilled and set. After both rivets are in place, the seam is set up tight with a wooden mallet and then smoothed with a planishing hammer.

dirt is hammered into the copper, and later, when the sheet is being prepared for brazing, it presents a difficult cleaning job.

**Thin Edging and Rolling Sheets.**—The preparation for the brazing and laying up of seams is very important. It must be done correctly, or almost certainly brazing trouble or even complete failure will be the result. Figure 40 shows a sheet being thin-edged, rolled, and riveted in preparation for brazing. Part 1 shows how the sheet is thin-edged for spelter brazing. Opposite sides are thin-edged, so that the tapered wedges will fit smoothly when put together, leaving a surface without lumps. Part

2 shows the rolling operation done with hand tools. The copper sheet should be annealed before being rolled. Roll both ends first near the thin edge and then bend the middle. Roll the copper so that it holds together by itself, one seam pressing against the other, before riveting it. Drill one end for riveting, drive the rivet, and then take all slack out from both sheets by hammering on a mandrel with a mallet (see part 3). Drill the other end, and drive the second rivet. Close the seam tightly against the mandrel with a planishing hammer. When the seam is tight, move the sheet so that the open end of the seam lies on top of the mandrel; then hammer on the section next to the open end of the seam. This will put a tension on the inner part of the seam, thus aiding the next step, brazing.

Any one of the foregoing points, if omitted, may be a contributing factor to sheet-brazing failure. The best possible care must be taken to secure a good thin edge, a thorough cleaning, rolling with the proper tension, clean rivets, the proper lay up, and a good fluxing.

**Brazing Sheets.**—When a braze is begun, all the necessary equipment should be ready: borax, spelter, spelter spoon, holding-up bar, poker or light bar for inside, two pairs of large tongs for holding the work steady, and pieces of pipe to slip over tongs for clamping tongs onto the copper. If you are using a kerosene forge, make certain that there is enough kerosene to complete the job during one continuous heat (because if the heat is shut off while the braze is still unfinished, the cooling action will oxidize the cleaned seam, making recleaning necessary for further successful brazing).

Figure 41 shows a brazing setup for sheet work. Large work to be brazed is hung on a swinging chain hoist so that it may be moved easily while being brazed. When the job to be brazed is hanging level and ready, the seam should be flushed thoroughly with borax and water solution, tapping along the seam very lightly so that the borax solution flushes the length of the seam. (The borax and water solution is usually mixed with the spelter and keeps the spelter thoroughly fluxed and ready for use.)

Charge the seam with just enough spelter to fill it. Too often seams are overcharged with spelter, and so a thick layer of excess spelter remains inside the job and usually has to be removed anyway. It is best to put on the spelter sparingly, adding more when necessary. Powdered borax is sprinkled on the spelter before brazing. If more spelter is necessary, it should be added during the brazing.

When large sheets are being brazed over a forge, it is best to have two mechanics, one to watch the inside and the other to take care of the seam underneath. The man taking care of the inside will have a light bar or poker, so that when the spelter melts he may move the grains from the sides and see that no lumps remain on the seam, and, if more spelter or borax is necessary, he may add it. The two men should work together as a team; the man watching the inside should tell the man working underneath when the spelter is melted.

The man underneath should use a solid bar flattened on the end. This bar is used to keep the seam tight while it is being brazed, for when heated the seam will usually open. If this opening is very large, it should be pushed closed with the bar when the copper is red-hot. At times, when the spelter is already melted on the inside, it will not come through because the seam is too tight. In such a case, the man underneath should either press easily on the top side of the seam or jar the sheet slightly, well away from the seam. This treatment will usually draw the spelter through.

When the spelter melts and starts coming through, the man working the bottom should see to it that the seam is kept snug, and at the same time he should "rub" the spelter to the spots where it is needed. When the braze is finished, there should be a line of spelter showing through at the bottom.

The puddling, or holding-up, bar should be dipped into powdered borax occasionally. This will help to flux the bottom of the seam and at the same time aid the flow. Plenty of borax should be used in brazing the seams. It should be sprinkled on when the spelter is molten.

**Seam Lay-up Problems** (see Fig. 41).—Seam roll up and lay up is as important in sheet work as setup is in branch brazing. The figure shows three methods of forming the sheet. The reason for forming sheets in these various shapes is to relieve their tendency to warp when being brazed. The theory is that a flat sheet, when heated, warps and distorts visibly, but a cylinder or rounded surface does not. For this reason all flat places on the sheet are removed before it is brazed.

Small work made of heavy material is usually rolled into a round shape for brazing, whereas small work of thin material should be rolled into a pear shape. The pear shape is more satisfactory and is less likely to distort when heated.

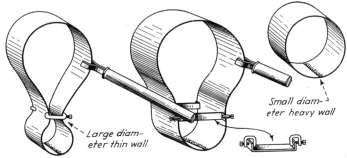

*Small diameter heavy wall*

*Large diameter thin wall*

Small work in heavy-gauge material is left round for brazing while the pear shape is best on large diameters

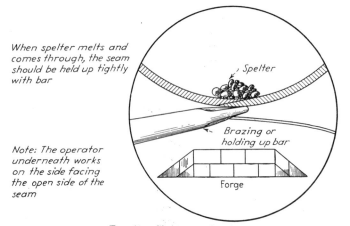

When spelter melts and comes through, the seam should be held up tightly with bar

*Spelter*

*Brazing or holding up bar*

Note: The operator underneath works on the side facing the open side of the seam

Forge

FIG. 41.—Sheet-seam brazing.

Thin work of large diameters is rolled into two loops, one large and one small, as shown in Fig. 41, and held together tightly with a clamp as an extra measure of precaution against distortion during the brazing.

Heavy metals may be rolled and held together in the pear shape, as shown in the diagram, with a piece of flat iron and clamps. Ordinarily the flat bar and the clamp arrangement are not necessary, but they may be used as an extra precaution.

It should be understood that when the work is in the process of being brazed, the metal becomes very soft, and whatever handling is done must be very gentle; otherwise the seam may be be spread open, necessitating relaying up and recleaning in order to obtain good results.

The close-up of Fig. 41, showing the bar in operation while the metal is being brazed, demonstrates how this bar is used. The seam, when heated, has a tendency to open slightly; this bar is used to push the copper back into place. The bar should be handled lightly, or the seam may be completely distorted.

**Silver Brazing and Sheet Work.**—Silver brazing has not come into general use on sheet bends and sheet work because of the working, or the forming, necessary after the brazing has been completed. However, on many jobs where forming is not necessary, silver solder can be used advantageously.

**Advantages of Hammering Seams.**—There are two reasons for hammering seams. The first is to make a smooth, workmanlike job by hammering the seam to the same thickness as the sheet. The second is that, when the seam is hammered, it will stand more working and flexing because of the change that takes place in the structure of the spelter. This change, theoretically, is the same as that which takes place when cast brass is cold-rolled into a sheet. The sheet brass will stand more bending and working before it breaks or tears than the cast brass. So will the cold-hammered seam stand more working. Seams should never be worked hot, because the spelter (or brass) is short hot and will break or tear easily while hot.

**Making a Pipe from Two Spliced Sheets.**—When a pipe must be made from two sheets of copper because one sheet is too short to make the full length of the pipe, the two sheets are spliced transversely and then joined longitudinally. Here the practice of making the splice on an angle is an advantage, provided that the waste metal can be spared. The cutting and brazing are done on an angle so that, when the sheet is rolled for the final braze, only one side of the transverse seam at a time intersects the main seam during the brazing operation.

The size of the angle of splice is decided by the amount of metal that can be spared; for instance, a 6-in. taper will make the transverse seam 6 in. apart at the longitudinal. The idea is to space it so that, when the longitudinal is brazed, only one intersecting seam will be on the fire at a time.    In this way the chances of melting out the transverse seam are lessened.

**Rounding a Distorted Cylinder or Pipe on a Mandrel.**—Select a mandrel as near the diameter of the cylinder as is available. Anneal the cylinder first, and then round it up as well as possible with hand tools.    When this is done, place the cylinder on the mandrel.    Hammer a complete course the full length of the cylinder solidly against the mandrel, and then move the cylinder 4 or 5 in. and repeat this operation.    Continue until a complete turn of the cylinder has been made.    The distance of the spacing while hammering the first time around depends on the diameter of the cylinder.    If the cylinder is 12 in. in diameter or larger, a 4- or 5-in. spacing would be enough, but, if the cylinder is smaller, the spacings might be started closer together.    Then hammer another course, dividing equally the space that was not hammered, and make another complete rotation.    Continue this operation until all the gaps have been hammered.    The cylinder should now be round if the hammering was fairly even. When rounding a cylinder that is made of sheet copper, always start the hammering away from the seam.

# CHAPTER XIV

## SHEET BENDS

Bends in pipe over 12 in. in diameter are made by forming two separate sheets (a throat piece and a back piece) and then brazing them together. Extremely sharp-radius bends of small-diameter pipe can also be done this way. The great advantage in making pipe bends by this method is that there is no stretching of the back or puckering of the throat as in rosin or sand bending. The metal thickness remains nearly constant except on the sides where the seams are, and there the back piece is thickened while the throat piece is thinned; thus the back piece compensates for the throat. This method of making bends requires no filling and no large bending machinery.

The work is done with hand tools and can be done in almost any shop that has an anglesmith's slab, large heating torches, and a forge. The necessary mallets may be made of oak, maple, or any good hardwood.

**Procedure.**—Lay out the copper sheets as shown in Fig. 42. The length of the back piece is measured on the back of the layout, and the length of the throat piece is measured on the center line of the layout. Add enough length to allow for the buckle, as shown in the throat-piece diagram.

**Working the Back Piece** (see Fig. 43).—The procedure in working the back piece is to bend the sheet to fit the slab layout and then to secure the sheet to the slab with a piece of angle bar, C clamps, and a slab dog, as shown. Bend over the ends and the straight section first. This will help to stiffen the sheet and will prevent vibration during the hammering. Bump back the section at the working line from $A$ to $B$. Next work the top of $AB$ toward the center line by hammering with mallets. This should be done while the copper is red-hot. Heat the job to a red heat and hammer it until cold; then heat it again, etc., until the job is finished.

When the top is worked over at the bend, the copper will wrinkle. These wrinkles must be hammered smooth before they become sharp and deep. Remove the wrinkles by heating them until red-hot and then hammer down on them with a small mallet while using a large mallet underneath as a bucker.   If they still

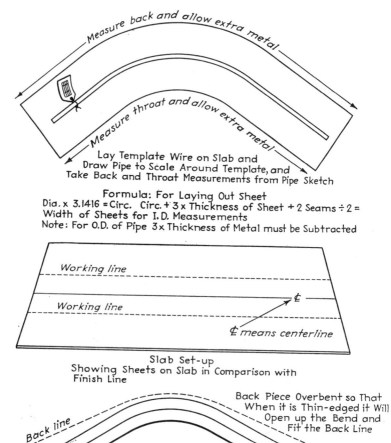

Measure back and allow extra metal

Measure throat and allow extra metal

Lay Template Wire on Slab and
Draw Pipe to Scale Around Template, and
Take Back and Throat Measurements from Pipe Sketch

Formula: For Laying Out Sheet
Dia. x 3.1416 = Circ.  Circ. + 3 x Thickness of Sheet + 2 Seams ÷ 2 =
Width of Sheets for I.D. Measurements
Note: For O.D. of Pipe 3 x Thickness of Metal must be Subtracted

Working line

Working line

℄

℄ means centerline

Slab Set-up
Showing Sheets on Slab in Comparison with
Finish Line

Back Piece Overbent so That
When it is Thin-edged it Will
Open up the Bend and
Fit the Back Line

Back line

Throat line

Throat Piece is Under-
bent so that thin Edging
Will Draw it Up to Throat Line

FIG. 42.—Sheet-bend layout.

are not smooth, they should be smoothed with a steel planishing hammer and a hand dolly or a steel head as a bucker.

Bend Ends over Before Working
Center Section
Bump Out from A to B on Working
Line and Work Back Over Hot

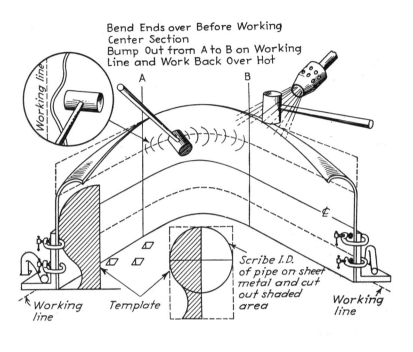

*Scribe I.D. of pipe on sheet metal and cut out shaded area*

Working line    Template    Working line

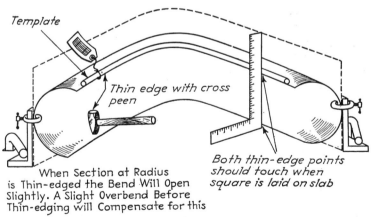

*Template*

*Thin edge with cross peen*

*Both thin-edge points should touch when square is laid on slab*

When Section at Radius
is Thin-edged the Bend Will Open
Slightly. A Slight Overbend Before
Thin-edging will Compensate for this

Fig. 43.—Working the back piece.

Use a sheet-metal template to check the shape of the half radius as the copper is being worked. When the copper is shaped to fit the sheet-metal template, the center-line template is tried on. It may be necessary to work the copper at $AB$ in order to fit the center-line template. This may be done by loosening one side of the sheet from the slab and closing or opening the bend as needed while heating and working the section requiring the change. When both the sheet-metal and the center-line template fit the work, the sheet is turned over and the other side is worked in a similar manner. A disc template for the inside diameter is made, and the sheet is formed to fit the radius of the disc.

Extreme care should be taken when you are setting up the sheet to work the second side so that the center line of the sheet measures the same distance up from the slab at both ends and throughout the sheet. Carelessness in setting up for the second side may develop a twisted bend, which is difficult to remedy. When both sides are worked over, the bend should be checked with a square, as shown in Fig. 43, so that both bottom and top of the seam edges will be touching the square when it is laid on the slab and against the worked-over ends.

**Working the Throat** (see Fig. 44).—Bend the sheet to fit the throat layout on the working slab; then buckle the sheet away from the throat layout line toward the center line at bend $AB$. This is done to allow the metal at the throat to be stretched but still to preserve the original thickness of the seam edge. When this is done, fasten the sheet to the slab as shown in Fig. 43 (backpiece).

Heat section $AB$ at the center line between working lines before bumping this section out to the throat line marked on the slab. When the center part is bumped out, heat the top and work it over toward the center line of the pipe; this will require stretching the metal instead of wrinkling it as in the back-piece. The straight section on the sides of the bend should be bent over as the throat is being worked. Do not bend the extreme ends over on the throat piece first as is done on the backpiece.

When one side is done, turn it over and finish the other side. Check to both the disc template and the center-line template; then prepare to thin-edge.

**Thin Edging.**—Before thin edging, lay the center-line template on the bend and mark the edge for trimming. The edge is usually slightly uneven and should be trimmed before being thin-edged. Trim the edge by sawing it with a hack saw or cut it with

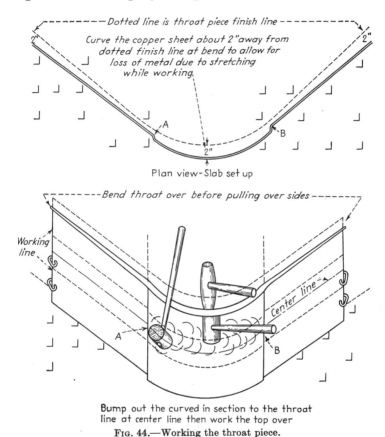

Plan view-Slab set up

Bump out the curved in section to the throat line at center line then work the top over

FIG. 44.—Working the throat piece.

a chisel while it rests solidly against a slab or anvil. Mark the part to be thin-edged with a pair of dividers (compass); then scribe a line into the copper so that it is easily visible during thin edging. Then thin-edge the seams from the inside with the copper resting against a smooth solid piece of steel such as an anvil or a slab edge.

Figure 42 shows the allowance method for the opening and closing of sheets during thin edging.

The matter of overbend and underbend is usually worked out according to the individual coppersmith's methods of working, since the amount of allowance for opening is a matter of experi-

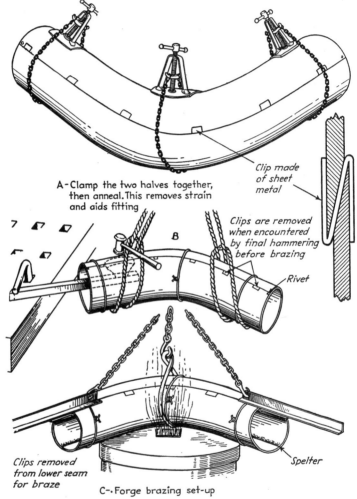

A-Clamp the two halves together, then anneal. This removes strain and aids fitting

Clip made of sheet metal

Clips are removed when encountered by final hammering before brazing

B

Rivet

Clips removed from lower seam for braze

C-.Forge brazing set-up

Spelter

FIG. 45.—Laying up and brazing sheet bends.

ence, depending on the radius of the bends and the thickness of the sheet.

**Fitting Back and Throat Together.**—After both the back and throat pieces have been thin-edged, they are fitted together, the seam of the throat piece fitting over the seam of the back. Small sheet-metal clips of black iron or burned galvanized iron are bent to the seam-lap measurement and placed at intervals on the seam (see Fig. 45A).

A clamp-and-chain device is placed on the pipe, pulling the sheets together. Care should be taken that when the sheets are pulled together the thin edge will not double over. When the sheets are set together fairly tight, heat is applied with torches, annealing both the back and the throat. When they are annealed, a flatter is used to tap together the places that do not quite fit. The clamping device is tightened wherever necessary. This procedure releases all strain and allows for the proper seam lap.

After being fitted, the sheets are taken apart, cleaned both with acid and mechanical methods, and set together again. After cleaning, use the clips again on the seams, wiring both parts together this time with heavy black-iron wire, as shown in *B*.

The pipe is then suspended as in *B*, with the seam drilled and riveted on one end. The seam is set on the hammering head as shown and laid together tightly with a wooden mallet by hammering the seam that is free of the clips. After the whole length of the seam has been laid up with the wooden mallet, the opposite end is drilled and riveted. The planishing hammer is used for final laying up, and the clips are removed as they are encountered. This seam is now ready for brazing. Work the other seam in a similar manner after brazing the first one.

**Brazing the Seam** (see Sheet Brazing).—Figure 41*C* shows a seam-brazing setup over a forge. The clamp arrangement is made of two pieces of angle iron bolted together and tightened onto the pipe. The hole in the top is for lifting with a chain. The ring shown at the center of the bend balances the setup; this ring is pushed aside slightly when one is brazing near it.

The pipe should be balanced so that the seam is level during the brazing process and not too heavily charged with spelter, as this will leave a thick, lumpy seam that will be difficult to hammer and work. The wires holding the bend together for brazing are easily broken off when they are heated; they are removed as the seam is being brazed near them by being pushed out of the way before the spelter flows through the seam.

The brazing operation is not started at the extreme end of the pipe. Start brazing about a foot or so from the end, and braze toward the near end first. When finished on one end, start brazing again where first begun and complete the opposite end of the pipe. After being brazed, the pipe is immersed in acid, washed with water, and dried with a torch. The unbrazed seam should be opened and cleaned, and the clips moved to clean the metal under them. After the seam is clean, the same method of laying up is used as on the first seam.

**Cleaning, Chipping, and Grinding.**—Most of the glazed borax is removed by the sulphuric acid bath; however, the remaining borax and lumps of spelter may be removed with a small portable grinder, chisels, and files. Care should be taken when using a grinder that the copper, as well as excess spelter, is not ground away.

**Hammering the Seam.**—After the seams are free of lumps and excess spelter, the pipe is either planished on a hammering head or hammered while under water pressure. In order to hammer the pipe while it is subjected to water pressure, it is necessary to have a pair of flanges on the pipe. A good practice is to Van Stone the flanges on and to remove them after hammering and testing.

# CHAPTER XV

## TESTING

Nearly all pipework is tested in the shop before being installed aboard ship. The testing pressure is generally about twice the operating pressure of the pipe. Small-diameter piping can withstand greater internal pressure than large-diameter piping of the same wall thickness. For this reason it is advisable to use great caution when testing large-diameter pipes or fittings. Pressures that would be insufficient for proper testing of a small pipe may cause large-diameter pipes to swell or burst.

When a pipe has sharp or distorted bends, it should be secured either by wiring or by installing a rigid bar to make certain that the bend will not move while the tube is subjected to water pressure (see Fig. 46). Theoretically, if a pipe is round, the bend will not move during testing, but in ordinary work the pipe is seldom round. See Fig. 46 for what might happen when distorted bends are tested.

**Water and Air Testing.**—Certain pipe lines require an air test besides the regular water test. Those recommended for the air test are gasoline, oil, and high- and low-pressure air lines. **Caution :** Lines must be entirely free of all traces of oil before they are tested with compressed air or oxygen. Oxygen and oil, are highly explosive. On these lines the water test is more or less a strength test. If a weak spot shows during the water test, water will squirt and nothing will be harmed except by the wetting. If, however, a line that is being tested with air is broken, it may be dangerous to persons near by because air under pressure is compressed, and parts of the metal from the pipe may be hurled by the force of the air. The compressed air itself is a powerful striking force. The water test should precede the air test whenever practicable.

Small leaks on pipe and castings that show in an air test will not show in a water test. In testing with air, the outside of the fitting, pipe, or casting is painted with a soap-and-water mixture.

If there are leaks, the escaping air will make bubbles, thus showing the spot that leaks.

**Blanks and Strong-backs.**—Testing blanks are made of solid-steel plates with boltholes drilled to suit the flange of the pipe to be tested.   A hole is drilled and tapped for a pipe fitting some-

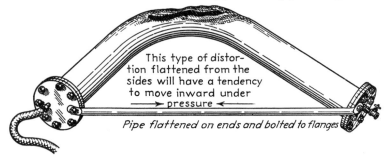

This type of distortion flattened from the sides will have a tendency to move inward under pressure

Pipe flattened on ends and bolted to flanges

Note: Anneal pipe at point of before subjecting to water pressure

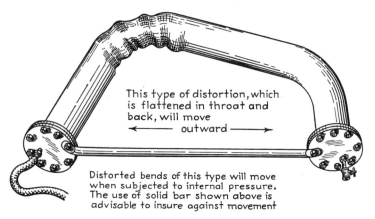

This type of distortion, which is flattened in throat and back, will move outward

Distorted bends of this type will move when subjected to internal pressure. The use of solid bar shown above is advisable to insure against movement

Fig. 46.—Removing distortions hydraulically.

where near the center of the blank.   Strong-backs are used on the larger diameter flanges to keep the blanks from bellying out, or distorting, during the test.   Strong-backs should be used on all pipes from about 10 in. I.P.S. on up, especially when thin-wall blanks are used (see Fig. 48).

**Water Test.**—Steel testing blanks are bolted onto the flanges; then a water hose or pipe is connected to a hole tapped in the blank on one end, while on the other blank a valve is installed for releasing the pressure and evacuating the air. The water is turned on and the pipe filled; to make sure that the air is completely excluded, raise the end of the pipe until the flange on the release side is horizontal. When the air stops spurting and a steady stream of water flows from the release valve, the release valve may be closed.

For temporary pipe-testing purposes, such as testing a large-sheet elbow after brazing it, a silver-brazing high-collar flange is suitable. It should be sweated on with soft solder to allow easy removal after testing. The nonsilver insert-type flange should be used unless only a silver insert flange is available. Then, of course, the silver ring should be removed before it is sweated onto the pipe.

**Removing Distortions and Dents by Water Pressure.**—Copper piping is often distorted by being crushed or dropped. When hand tools cannot be used to remove these dents and distortions, the use of water pressure is very often successful. The method is to anneal just the distorted part of the pipe, put on the test blanks, and then apply the water pressure. While the pipe is being subjected to water pressure, it should be hammered lightly, just around the dent. During the hammering, the dent will be seen to rise. If the dent is not removed completely with one operation, it should be annealed at the distortion and the operation repeated. This may have to be done several times in extreme cases.

On heavy-walled piping, the internal pressure used must be greater than on thin-walled piping. When using high pressures, take care not to exceed the bursting and swelling pressures of the pipe or fitting being tested.

**Hydraulic Rat.**—Although dents and distortions in copper piping may be easily removed by hand or water pressure, the same does not hold true with copper-nickel or steel piping, and so a means has been devised to remove dents and distortions.

Plungers of varying shapes, such as shown in Fig. 47, are forced through the pipe. A leather cup, fastened to the plunger, acts as a check valve, thus causing the water pressure to push the plunger through the pipe. These plungers are called "hydraulic rats," and they are easily made in all sizes. No up-to-date shop should be without them. The rat is forced through the pipe by

water pressure.    As it moves through the pipe, the depressions
or wrinkles are forced outward, and the size is rounded.    The
pressure necessary to push the rat through varies according to
the depth of the wrinkles and the thickness of side walls.    Care
should be taken when using this method of removing distortions

A- Hinge type          B- Ball bearing          C- Bullet type

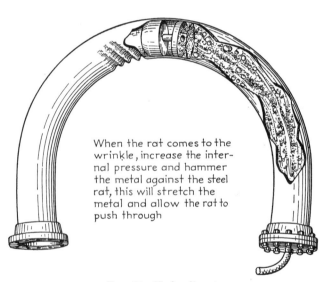

When the rat comes to the
wrinkle, increase the internal pressure and hammer
the metal against the steel
rat, this will stretch the
metal and allow the rat to
push through

Fig. 47.—Hydraulic rat.

with copper because the copper pipe diameters are easily enlarged
by the pressures required to drive the rat through the pipe.

The hydraulic rat is a steel plug that is machined to fit snugly
inside a pipe, with the front end rounded smoothly and the other
end flat, as in Fig. 47A and C.    A bolt that holds a cup leather
in place is centered in the flat end of the rat.

Ball bearings that fit snugly inside a pipe can be used instead of
a rat for small-diameter work.    In this case, rags that have been
thoroughly saturated in grease or oil are used instead of leathers

to form the gasket behind the ball. Rags are also a good substitute for the regular leathers on the large-sized rats. Rats made of hardwood can be used, but they are good only on well-annealed copper that is not too sharply indented. The wooden rats last for about one or two jobs.

Figure 47 shows the types of rat to use for removing dents and distortions from pipe. They are *A*, the hinged rat, *B*, the ball bearing, and *C*, the bullet type.

*D* shows *A* in operation. The hinged two-piece rat is best for sharp bends and may also be used on straight pipe; the bullet shape can be used on large-radius bends. When rounding a sharp bend in the pipe, the hinged rat bends and follows the curve of the pipe, whereas, if the solid type were used on sharp bends, it would have a tendency to open the sharp bends or to distort the shape of the back.

If the wrinkles are deep, the long, tapered bullet type may be used to advantage. The long taper gets a gradual purchase on the deep wrinkles as it travels through, forcing them upward gradually instead of with an abrupt right-angle push as it would with a blunt-shaped rat.

The rat will move freely through the pipe with a minimum of water pressure until it strikes the wrinkle; then it will stop, and the pressure will have to be increased to force it through. If the wrinkle is sharp, as shown, the rat will freeze solid. In this case, the pipe should be hammered directly against the side of the steel rat at the high point of the wrinkle, stretching the pipe by the impact of the hammer against the steel rat inside, while the pressure is increased internally against the rat. This treatment will usually succeed if enough internal pressure is used.

If the wrinkles are very deep and the bend extremely sharp, especially on copper or copper nickel, the rat may not remove the wrinkles when passing through. It may only push out the back of the bend, distorting it or breaking through the metal. The rat, of course, can be of aid only if the wrinkles or depressions are reasonably shallow. There is no gauge to tell just how much pressure will be necessary to remove the wrinkles, because no two situations are ever exactly alike.

It makes no difference on which part of the pipe the distortion may be; it can be removed provided that the wrinkle or distortion is not too sharp and deep.

**Testing Large Expansion Joints.**—Figure 48 shows a setup for testing an expansion joint with water pressure before it is

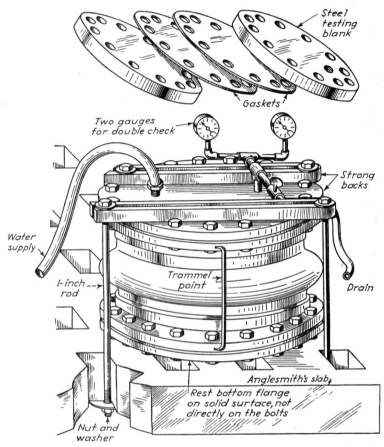

The strong backs in this case serve
a double purpose
1- To keep blank flanges from bowing out
2- To secure expansion joint to slab and
   prevent it from opening up under pressure

Fig. 48.—Testing expansion joints.

installed. If pressure were injected into an expansion joint that was not prepared to withstand the pressure, the joint would become distorted. It is so flexible that the water pressure would open it like an accordion.

First, the proper-size blanks are placed on the joint that is to be tested. These blanks should be made of steel and should be ¾ to 1 in. thick with a hole tapped in the plate (or blank) somewhere near the center of the flat surface for a ½- or ⅜-in. pipe. Place a thick cardboard or rubber gasket on the face of the flange and lay the blank on top. Bolt the blank onto the flange.

Tighten the bolts gradually, working the bolts snug diametrically opposite to each other and completing the whole circle of bolts. This prevents distortion of the flange. **Do not fully tighten the bolts when first putting them on.** Make several complete circles, gradually tightening the bolts each time around.

When both blanks have been tightened securely, lay the joint on an anglesmith's slab or its equivalent. Place a plate between the blank and the slab in such a manner that the bolts do not rest against the slab; this prevents bowing of the blank when the pressure is turned on.

Next, lay strong-backs across the face of the blank and bolt them to the anglesmith's slab. The strong-backs are used to prevent the top blank from bowing out and to prevent the expansion joint from opening. Make at least three trammel-point markings on the flanges. Trammel-point markings will be a check on whether or not the joint has moved during the test. Trammel points can be made of ⅜-in. round or square steel bent over at right angles on both ends and pointed.

Next, screw the necessary pipe fittings and double gauges into the tapped opening in the blank; also connect a bleed-off valve to this gauge arrangement. Screw a water hose into the bottom blank, if you can get to it; if not, make another tapped opening in the top blank. Open the release and water valves. Fill the expansion joint with water; when it is full, water will flow from the release valve in a full, steady stream.

Watch the gauges and close the release valve down until the gauges show the required amount of pressure. Large expansion joints are tested from about 25 to 50 lb. per sq. in. Do not allow the pressure to exceed the required test pressure specified for the job. Make sure that the gauges check when the pressure starts to rise. If they do not check, one of them is out of adjustment. Remove both of them and have them calibrated, or get new gauges.

After the required pressure is attained, examine both flanges, the brazed seams, etc., for possible leaks.   If no leaks are found, release the pressure by turning off the supply valve and then dismantle the setup.   Remove the gauges, strong-backs, blanks, and check the trammel-point markings.   If the trammel-point markings check, anneal the expansion joint and prepare it for shipment.   If a trammel-point discrepancy exists, it must be corrected after annealing either by forcing the flanges apart slightly or by forcing them together, depending on which is needed.

**Testing Expansion Joints (Bellows Type).**—When an expansion joint is prepared for testing, strips of heavy-gauge copper should be soldered or silver soldered at several points inside the joint, bridging the bellows opening.   These strips will aid in preventing the joint from opening when internal pressure is injected.   They should be removed after the test is completed.

# CHAPTER XVI

## MISCELLANEOUS

Bosses are bronze or brass castings that are drilled and tapped; they are then secured to the sides of pipes or fittings and used as connections to which screwed pipes or plugs may be fitted. Although there are many kinds, they may be classified into two groups, the surface boss and the imbedded boss.

**Surface Boss.**—The surface boss is the type most commonly used. It may be brazed with either spelter or silver. Spelter is preferable if the job is to be done in the shop, but, if fabrication is to be done aboard ship, the silver braze is easier because it requires less heat.

The surface boss must be fitted by cutting, grinding, or filing to the shape of the pipe to which it will be brazed; a snug fit must be made between the pipe and the boss before brazing. Before the surface boss is spelter brazed, it is fitted, cleaned, wired to the pipe, fluxed with borax, and surrounded by a mud dam of $\frac{1}{2}$ in. or so to hold the spelter. In silver brazing, the mud is not needed, and the silver flux should be applied before the boss is wired to the pipe; otherwise the procedure is similar to spelter brazing.

**Imbedded Bosses.**—The imbedded boss is fitted into an opening that has been made on the pipe or fitting, peened, and then brazed like a cup joint (see Fig. 16). Whenever a long boss is needed, the coppersmith can save material by fitting a short piece of boss material into a branch, either into a cup branch or into a saddle branch, instead of using a long piece of solid boss material. The imbedded type used in the end of a branch has advantages over the solid-metal boss, because it is light in weight, quicker to make, and can more easily be made to fit onto the pipe curves.

When preparing an imbedded boss for brazing, grind or file a small groove completely around its side, and calk it into the cup to prevent it from falling through when heat expands the copper during the brazing.

**Bosses for Thermometer Wells.**—When thermometer wells are needed in small-diameter pipe lines, there are two general methods of making the bosses. As shown on Fig. 49, the boss fitted into a branch gives the required length on the side of a pipe.

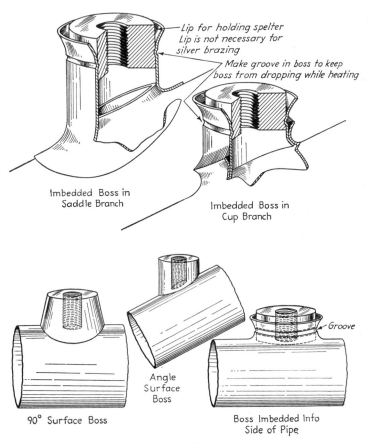

FIG. 49.—Bosses.

This is necessary because the thermometer well extends down into the pipe itself, and on small pipes, if this length is not added, the well would touch the back of the pipe. This would either break the well or prevent it from being screwed down sufficiently. Another way to allow well room is to use a larger pipe and to reduce both ends. This also ensures a full flow of liquids.

**General Information on Bosses.**—If the boss material is made of high-melting-point brazing metal, the bosses may be either spelter brazed or silver brazed; but if they are made of low-melting yellow brass, they must be brazed with silver solder. In emergencies, the cup type may be tinned and sweated if brazing materials are not available.

Surface bosses may be put on straight or on angles, depending on the work, although, if extreme angles are desired, the branch boss is easier and quicker to install. Imbedded bosses have their special uses when a long boss is needed or when boss material is scarce. The boss is imbedded and brazed into a cup formed either in the side of the pipe or in a branch.

TABLE XVI.—BRAZING BOSSES

| No. | O.D., in. | I.P.S., in. |
|---|---|---|
| 2 | 1 | $\frac{1}{8}$–$\frac{1}{4}$–$\frac{3}{8}$ |
| 5 | $1\frac{5}{8}$ | $\frac{1}{2}$–$\frac{3}{4}$ |
| 8 | $1\frac{7}{8}$ | 1 |
| 11 | $2\frac{1}{8}$ | $1\frac{1}{4}$ |
| 14 | $2\frac{1}{2}$ | $1\frac{1}{2}$ |

**Copper-nickel Alloy.**—An alloy composed of approximately 30 per cent nickel and 70 per cent copper is now being used extensively in shipbuilding. It is used almost entirely in the form of tubing. The tubes, after being bent to the required shapes, have flanges fitted to them and then are installed aboard ship.

Copper-nickel is supposed to be highly resistant to electrolysis, or galvanic action. The use of a copper-nickel alloy seems to be the answer to the many leaks and troubles that have caused shutdowns in the machinery aboard ship. Copper-nickel is white, like nickel.

**Uses.**—In general, copper-nickel is used on salt-water lines, where it is replacing lead-lined piping and tinned and wiped copper.

**Acid for Cleaning Copper-nickel.**—The copper-nickel alloy is cleaned with full-strength muriatic acid, either by swabbing or by immersion.

**Working and Bending Characteristics.**—Copper-nickel has the working characteristics of copper. Successful working of a copper-nickel alloy can be done only while the metal is cold. Copper-nickel is a short-hot metal, meaning that it will break or tear if worked while hot.

General meaning of "working" is hammering, bending, stretching, reducing, or flexing, in fact, anything done to the metal that changes its shape. The amount of working to be done between annealings is difficult to determine, as it depends on individual jobs, situations, and handling of the metal by the mechanic.

Some causes of failure in the working of copper-nickel are working it while it is hot, working it too long between annealings, and allowing wrinkles to become sharp and deep.

**Preheating Copper-nickel.**—When "tacking" branches or flanges onto a pipe for fitting purposes, apply the heat carefully. If only one small spot is heated, it will expand excessively, creating a terrific strain on the heated point and surrounding area. This is likely to crack the branch, which is already slightly thinned from being worked. The proper way to tack a copper-nickel branch or flange is to heat the complete circumference first, then, when it is well preheated, to apply the heat to the local points where the tack is to be.

This practice of preheating should be applied to any job where heat is needed on copper-nickel. The point to remember is that a large surface should be heated before brazing heat is applied to any one point.

**Bending a Copper-nickel Pipe with Rosin Filling.**—Rosin filling in copper-nickel piping is considered the best aid in bending large-diameter pipe at sharp radii. The method of bending is similar to that of bending copper pipe. (See Rosin Bending, Chap. X.) Do not allow wrinkles to become sharp; stop bending and hammer them out. Remove the rosin, anneal the pipe, refill with rosin, and then rebend.

**Sand Bending a Copper-nickel Pipe.**—Small tubing up to about 1 in. I.P.S. can be bent while sand filled. The bending is done cold, and either a press or a bending machine is used. Properly fitting dies are very important. The radius of the bend, of course, is limited to the radius of the die used. When sharp bending is required on small tubing, rosin is considered a better filling to use.

**Brazing Copper-nickel.**—Most brazing of copper-nickel is done with Grades III and IV silver solder. Grade V is used when a filler is required; it has a long melting-flowing range and can be controlled while building up or filling gaps in work that, for some reason, is poorly fitted. Spelter-silver combinations are also good for brazing copper-nickel, but, when the copper-zinc content is too high, it loses its resistance to salt-water action. Therefore silver solder is most satisfactory for copper-nickel piping.

Silver-solder flux is used on all silver-brazing work. However, when copper-nickel or steel is being worked, the flux should be of a thicker consistency than that used on copper.

**General Information on Copper-nickel.**—The melting point is about 2200°F., and the annealing point 1450°F. Clean with muriatic acid and tin with Spear Flux. Rubber-lined or asbestos hangers are used to retard electrolysis or galvanic action. Copper nickel is a very poor heat conductor, since it heats very similarly to steel; *i.e.*, if heat is applied to one part, it will turn red without the rest becoming even warm. For this reason, in the brazing of large surfaces, it is necessary either to apply the flame over a large area or use a larger torch with a soft flame to preheat the metal.

**Making a Copper Ball.**—Copper floats in various sizes and thickness of metals are often made by the coppersmith. The hand method of manufacture still prevails over modern spinning methods because usually only one ball of a certain size is needed at a time. If many of one size were needed, it would be cheaper, of course, to establish mass-production methods and to make the balls by the spinning method. It is, then, necessary for the coppersmith to be able with hand tools to make a ball to individual specifications.

Figure 50 shows the layout for making a ball. Enough metal is added to the layout for the seam. If the butt seam is used, no allowance is necessary. However, it is always worth while to add a little to allow for metal worked slightly off-center.

After the sheet is cut to size, it should be annealed, cooled, and then puckered as shown. If small thin-gauge balls are made, the sheet puckering is done on a piece of wood that has a *V* cut into the end or on a small bar; use a small wooden mallet. The puckers are laid into the sheet to make it easier to hammer. They should not be allowed to become too deep, or they will be difficult to hammer, and the danger of lapping over is greater. If lapping over occurs, the wrinkles will break the metal, ruining

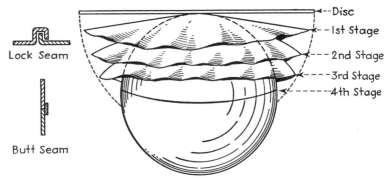

Lock Seam

Butt Seam

Disc

1st Stage

2nd Stage

3rd Stage

4th Stage

Formula: Radius of Ball X 3.1416, Plus Seam,
Equals Size of Disc

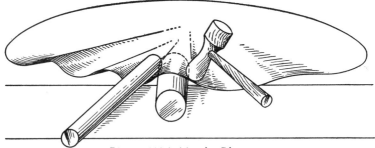

Place Wrinkles in Disc

Working the Ball
Over Steel Head

Rotate the Sheet
as Metal is Worked

Planishing

Fig. 50.—Making a ball out of sheet copper.

the sheet. The skill of working the wrinkles comes from experience and close observation. Heavy-gauge copper is less likely to wrinkle deeply than thin gauge.

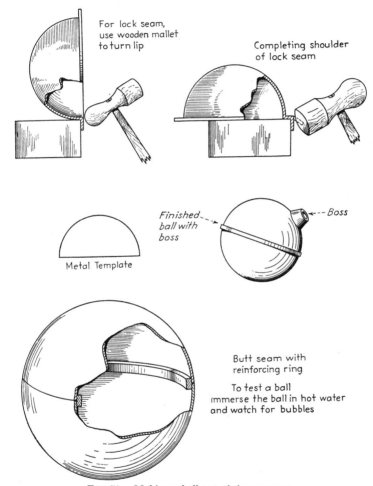

For lock seam, use wooden mallet to turn lip

Completing shoulder of lock seam

Metal Template

Finished ball with boss

Boss

Butt seam with reinforcing ring

To test a ball immerse the ball in hot water and watch for bubbles

FIG. 51.—Making a ball out of sheet copper.

Approximate operations of working a half ball from a sheet are shown in Fig. 50, which shows the shape the sheet takes during the hammering operations. Several intermediate annealings may be necessary in order to work the copper into its final shape. A sheet-metal or cardboard template is made to fit the inside of the ball in order to check the required shape during the working operations.

Figures 50 and 51 show the working operations. A wooden mallet is used when the copper is worked, the metal being held on a ball or steel head. If heavy material is being worked, it should be red-hot, being reheated whenever it cools. Tongs may be used to hold it on the ball. Revolve the sheet as it is being hammered; start near the center of the ball and work in circular courses until the end of the sheet is reached. If you are working the sheet cold, you should anneal it after each complete course.

When the sheet has been worked into a half ball and is ready for planishing, it should be slightly smaller than is required for the finished product, because of the stretching that takes place during planishing. The planishing is done to give a finished appearance to the work and also to harden the copper.

The seams are made to suit the work. In some cases a smooth-surfaced ball is needed; this is achieved by butting the seams together, using a reinforcing ring on the inside, and brazing both halves together. When the balls will have contact with salt water, they are tinned and lock seamed together and then soldered with a soldering iron.

A boss for threaded fittings is usually brazed or riveted to one of the half balls before the seams are tinned or brazed.

**Dovetail Patches.**—A dovetail patch is fitted and brazed in such a way that it has a smooth, imperceptible finish when completed. The material of the patch must be of the same thickness as that of the pipe. Figure 52 shows the dovetail patch in its various stages.

*A* shows the hole to be patched after it has been thin-edged and is ready for measuring. The thin edging is done by holding the copper on a steel bar or a suitable head and hammering with a bumping hammer or cross hammer. (See Thin-edging Chart for proper thin-edge lap, Fig. 39.)

*B* shows the operation of marking the patch, after the hole is thin-edged. Trim the patch so that after it is thin-edged it will fit on the thin-edged hole, making the required lap.

*C* shows cut dovetails. Dovetails should be cut so that they will lift from alternate sides. Cut the dovetails with a sharp chisel on an angle, to the depth of the hole diameter, so that the dovetail cut itself resembles a thin-edged lap. Do not cut the dovetails too deeply, thereby causing a gap that will weaken the patch. After the dovetails are cut, thin-edge them completely

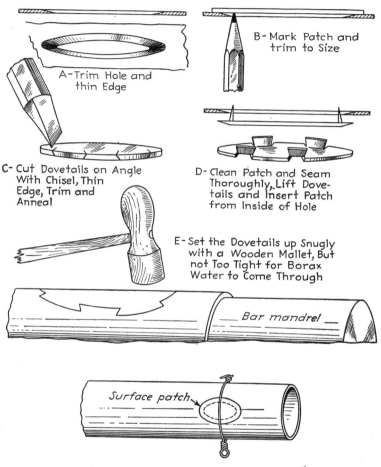

A-Trim Hole and thin Edge

B-Mark Patch and trim to Size

C- Cut Dovetails on Angle With Chisel, Thin Edge, Trim and Anneal

D- Clean Patch and Seam Thoroughly, Lift Dovetails and Insert Patch from Inside of Hole

E- Set the Dovetails up Snugly with a Wooden Mallet, But not Too Tight for Borax Water to Come Through

_Bar mandrel_

_Surface patch_

Surface Patches are Generally Made About $\frac{1}{2}"$ to 1" Larger Than the Hole to be Patched, They Can be Either Silver or Spelter Brazed, Whichever is the Most Practical. Patches Can Even be Soldered and Sweated in an Emergency

Fig. 52.—Patches.

around the patch. Then anneal it and lift the dovetails, as shown in *D*. Anneal and clean the dovetails and the thin-edged pipe and file or cut away all rough, ragged edges. Fit the dovetail patch into the hole from the inside whenever possible and then set the dovetails down smoothly with a wooden mallet while the work rests on a mandrel. Do not set the dovetails down so tightly that borax water cannot go through, because spelter will go only where the borax is. The capillary action of borax and heat draws the spelter. The spelter is usually placed on the inside, not on the outside, of the cylinder when a dovetail patch is brazed, because excess spelter on the outside has to be dressed off before hammering. The less spelter on the outside, the neater the job will be.

After the brazing is done, dress away all lumps of spelter and borax and then lay the work on a mandrel and hammer the patch to a smooth finish. The resulting job should be smooth and imperceptible, with only a pencil line of spelter showing on the surface.

Dovetail seams are also used in the making or patching of round-bottomed kettles, or on work where a smooth finish is desired. For best results dovetail patches should be brazed with spelter.

**Surface Patches** (see Fig. 52).—Surface patches are used to patch holes in pipe. The surface patch is a very common type of patch and may be brazed either with spelter or silver alloy, or it may be soldered. Patch the pipe with material as thick as or even thicker than the pipe walls. Cut the patch larger than the opening, fit it, wire it in place, and braze it on.

Spelter brazing is the best if annealing or working is to be done afterward. Brazing with silver solder is simplest, and the patch may be easily fitted and brazed onto the pipe while it is in place on the ship, as well as being brazed in the shop. Therefore, silver brazing is considered the best method.

Soft solder may also be used to hold the patch in an emergency, when brazing equipment is not available or when intense heat cannot be used safely. The patch may be put on with half-and-half solder, but, since solder is not so strong as spelter or silver, it should be reinforced by riveting and sweating. Riveted and sweated patches make a stronger job, but the ordinary sweat patch is good if plenty of lap is allowed in order to give it strength or especially if it is used on low-pressure systems.

**Pipe Hangers.**—Although there are many individual problems connected with supporting pipe aboard ship, it is not intended to cover all these problems here. The installation of hangers depends entirely on the local situation and the specifications regarding the work being done. The different systems require

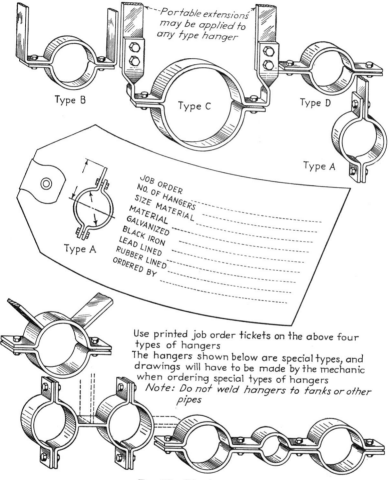

Fig. 53.—Pipe hangers.

special types of hangers made of different metals and with different linings. The most frequently used types of hangers are shown in Fig. 53.

The button-type hanger, which is not shown, is used on small tubing, ½ in. in diameter and smaller. It consists of a small clip that fits over the pipe and is screwed to a button that is welded to the bulkhead. The hanger is usually fitted snugly against the bulkhead and is similar to the hangers that electricians use to support cables. These hangers may be either the single- or double-button type, and sometimes they are made to accommodate several pipes grouped together.

The hangers used on copper pipe are lined with lead or compressed asbestos packing; those used on copper-nickel or tinned and wiped pipes are lined with rubber or compressed asbestos to insulate the pipe from the ship as well as to protect the pipe. The electrolytic action should be controlled wherever possible. Copper pipe that carries salt water is also protected from this action by rubber-lined hangers, thus preventing metal-to-metal contact.

Galvanized hangers are used on the top deck, bilges, and refrigerating units, where they are exposed to salt-water spray and corrosive action. When galvanized metal is unavailable, the coppersmith sometimes tins the hangers.

Many pipes need portable hangers to facilitate removal and emergency repairs. These are made by welding stubs to the ship's structure and then using bolts to fasten the hangers to the stubs. Type *C* hanger (see Fig. 53) shows the portable stubs that are welded to the overhead or to the bulkhead. This portable stub may be applied to all hanger types.

Some hangers are welded to the ship's structure; others are fastened with screws or bolts to the flanges of other piping or to machinery; some must be fastened so that they will vibrate with the machinery; others are solid and free of vibrating machinery. Expansion bends and expansion joints must be suspended so that the joints are left free to serve the purpose for which they are intended. Hangers are usually welded to beams, bulkheads, and overhead. They are sometimes welded to the skin of the ship, but this should be done only with the special permission of the supervisor.

Hangers should always be made as short as possible in order to prevent excessive vibration and the waste of material. Hanger legs are left either straight or twisted, as the job demands.

The hangers should be ordered so that they arrive on the job simultaneously with the finished pipe and can be installed at the same time. When order tickets for hangers are available, their use is recommended to facilitate ordering of hangers. Special types of hangers must be sketched and ordered when the individual jobs require it.

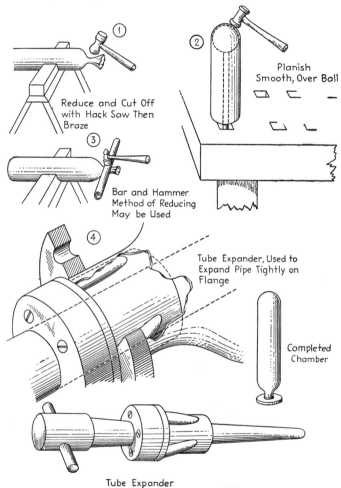

Reduce and Cut Off with Hack Saw Then Braze

Planish Smooth, Over Ball

Bar and Hammer Method of Reducing May be Used

Tube Expander, Used to Expand Pipe Tightly on Flange

Completed Chamber

Tube Expander

Fig. 54.—Making an air chamber.

**Making an Air Chamber.**—The coppersmith makes various shapes and types of air chambers of copper or alloy metals. The most common type of air chamber is made of copper tubing, with the ends reduced and the flange spelter brazed or silver brazed (see Fig. 54).

The method of manufacture is to reduce one end completely, to cut off the excess copper, and then to close the hole. If the work is to be spelter brazed, drill a hole in the closed end large enough to allow for a copper rivet of about $\frac{3}{16}$ or $\frac{1}{4}$ in. diameter, loose fit. Place the rivet in the hole with the head inside; apply borax and spelter, and then braze over a forge or with a torch, with the closed end of the chamber in a downward position. The spelter should flow through the space around the rivet.

After brazing, remove the surplus rivet and spelter and planish the head over a ball, as shown. After being planished smoothly, the opposite end should be reduced to the size of the flange used.

Figure 54 shows how to use a tube expander when expanding the copper inside a spelter-brazing flange preparatory to brazing. This flange may be spelter or silver brazed with equally good results. The tube expander is handy for work on small-sized pipe, where the ordinary method of calking with a ball-peen hammer or calking tools is awkward.

**Operation of Tube Expander.**—The tube expander has three small rollers that run freely in slots cut into the sides of a small cylinder. These rollers move outward when the loose tapered pin is inserted into the hole of the cylinder. When the pin is moved inward, the rollers are pushed against the tube sides; then the pin should be turned with a right-hand motion, which will start the cylinder rotating, moving the rollers tightly against the copper. This rotating motion will expand the copper as the rolls and pin travel inward. To release the roll from the tube, revolve the pin in the opposite direction.

**Knife-edge Union** (see Fig. 55).—The knife-edge union is used on high-pressure air lines. The copper ferrule $A$ is brazed onto the heavy high-pressure air line $B$. In tightening, brass nut $C$ draws copper ferrule $A$ against brass union $D$, grooving the harder knife-edged brass into the soft copper. This joint and the complete system are tested at a 5,000-lb. water pressure; the working pressure is about 2,000 lb. of air.

The brazing is done with spelter or spelter rod, using acetylene or with gas heat. Special care must be taken that penetration of the spelter is perfect, *i.e.* that it flows through the complete depth and on the face, filling the entire groove between the ferrule and the pipe.

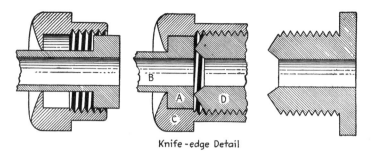

Knife -edge Detail

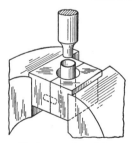

Make Sure That Spelter Runs
Through Completely Around.
File Face and Sides Clean of Spelter

Braze and fill
trough with
spelter

Peen with
center punch

File back of
ferrule to a
square shoulder

Spelter penetration

FIG. 55.—Knife-edge high-pressure union.

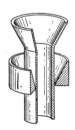

Flaring punch and die

1- Anneal copper tubing
2- Slip on nut and steel ring
3- Insert tube into die
4- Flare out with belling
   tool

Bell joint

After flaring the tube,
file off all burrs and uneven edges. Leave
enpugh copper to pro-
trude slightly above the
ring

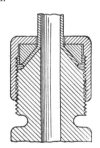

The flare should be
annealed, all burrs shoulc
be removed and blown
out with compressed air
before making up.
Grease the ring, nut,
and bell before instal-
ling

FIG. 56.—Bell or cone union.

**Bell Joints.**—Bell joints, another type of union, fit metal to metal with no gasket used. Figure 56 shows the joint and the method of manufacture. The type shown is used on modern high-pressure installations. There are many variations of the type shown, but the principle of the joint and the method of manufacture in each case are similar.

**Threading Copper Pipe.**—At times it is necessary to thread copper pipes, but because of the difficulty encountered when threading and the generally unsatisfactory results on high pressures, the method is not recommended if the pipe sections can be joined in any other way.

To thread copper it must be hard-rolled and not annealed. Soft copper will gum, and the threads will tear if threading is attempted; therefore, if annealed copper must be used, it must first be hardend. For best results, threaded copper joints should be tinned and sweated together.

**Riveted Seams.**—Many jobs and situations still require that seams be riveted. In most riveted jobs the seam and rivets are tinned and sweated together to ensure a leakproof joint. Riveted seams may be used on various jobs, especially where the pressures are low, but it is not advisable to use them on steam installations because the expansion and contraction caused by heating and cooling off has a tendency to crack the solder in the seams, thus causing leaks.

When a rivet-seamed tank is being made, the copper of the cylinder body need not be annealed. It may be left hard and the forming done on sheet rolls. After being formed, the seams are clamped together and then drilled. The size of the rivets used and the length of the seam lap are shown in the formula in Fig. 57. Always tin the rivets and the rivet holes and seams before riveting. Round-headed rivets are generally used because they are stronger, but in many cases the flat-headed, smooth-surface type serves the purpose better. A bucking head, or dolly, is used to hold the rivet solid while the rivet sets, "draw" and "button" are being applied. To ensure a tightly riveted seam, the seams and rivets are tinned. It will be found that after tinning both the rivets and the rivet holes, the rivets will not fit. The holes are then enlarged with a drift pin and the rivets inserted. The tinned rivets are driven into the tinned holes, the sheets are set together tightly, and the rivets are driven down. After the seam is riveted, it is fluxed and heated and filled with solder, care being taken that all the rivets have a coating of solder.

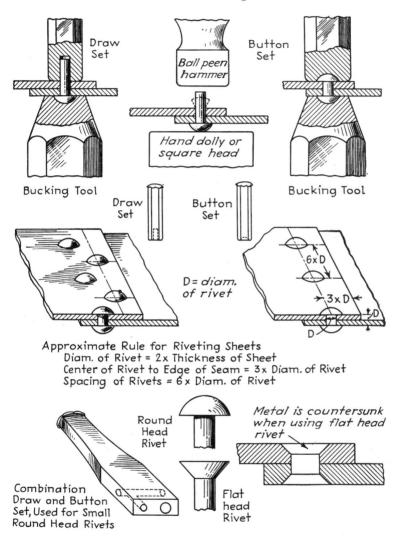

FIG. 57.—Riveted seams.

One of the advantages of the riveted and sweated seam appears in the making of a cylindrical tank with concave and convex heads. The bottom, or concave, head is the weak point on the tank, and for this reason it must be hammered (planished) until very hard before it is installed. If the head were brazed, the heat would anneal it; then, when internal pressure was injected, the bottom would bulge outward. Riveted and sweated seams have proved to be superior in this case because the copper retains its full temper after it is riveted and sweated.

**Correcting Inaccurately Aligned Boltholes.**—A slight misalignment of boltholes on the flanges of copper pipe can be corrected if the lengths are long enough. This is done by dogging one end to a slab, or holding tightly to one end, while twisting the other end. Two bolts are inserted in the flange diametrically opposite each other; then a flat bar is inserted between the bolts. The pipe should be·heated to a red heat, a strain taken on the flange, with the flat bar used as a lever, and the boltholes twisted into alignment. The heat should not be applied close to the flange. Short sections of pipe are difficult to work with, especially on large-diameter pipes. In that case, it is better to remove the flange and refit it. If the pipe is twisted too much, it may flatten out. When twisting the pipe, the coppersmith should observe the heated section very closely and stop twisting before the pipe begins to distort.

**Special Fittings.**—The use of copper fittings instead of castings is becoming more and more important in the repair and construction of ships. Many times it is possible to use copper salvaged from old or distorted pipe as material for special fittings. This is possible because of the ductility of copper and because copper does not deteriorate with age or use.

Special and individual fittings are quickly and easily made by the coppersmithing method because only one man is required to follow a job through to completion, but the castings necessary to serve the same purpose require more operations and more men, since the castings must go through several shops before they are ready for use.

Figure 58 shows a few instances where a cast fitting can be replaced by a copper fitting. Flanges for these fittings might be obtained from stock, or old salvaged flanges might be used. A cross fitting (shown in Fig. 58) can be made of copper by fitting two branches onto a straight piece of pipe. Either saddle branches or cup branches may be used. Many times the cross fitting itself is not needed at all, and the two branches installed in a long length of pipe eliminate the use of two flanges. Large cross fittings can be made from sheet copper.

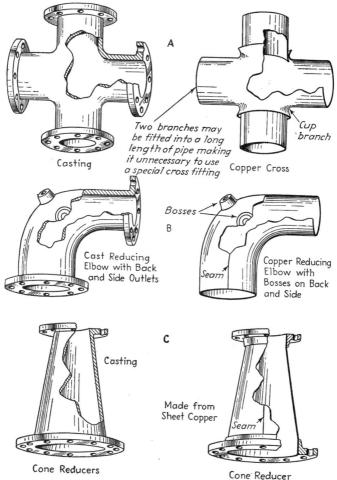

Fig. 58.—Handmade crosses and ells.

Reducing ells (Fig. 58*B*), and ordinary ells can be made to suit, with bosses and branches on them. (See Sheet Bends, Chap. XIV.)

Cones (Fig. 58*C*) of any dimension can easily be made of sheet copper and flanged to suit.

Excellent Y fittings of any dimensions (Fig. 59) may be made from sheet copper or copper pipe. The larger diameters are made of sheet metal similar to sheet bends. Smaller Y's are made from pipe, as shown.

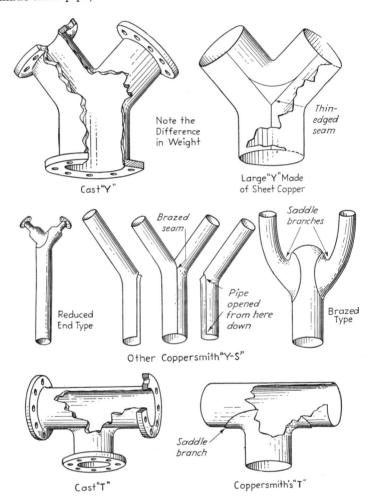

Note the Difference in Weight

Cast"Y"

Thin-edged seam

Large"Y"Made of Sheet Copper

Reduced End Type

Brazed seam

Pipe opened from here down

Saddle branches

Brazed Type

Other Coppersmith"Y-S"

Cast"T"

Saddle branch

Coppersmith's"T"

Fig. 59.—Handmade Y's and T's.

Another reason why fittings are coming into greater favor is the saving of metals involved. A special fitting made of copper weighs about half as much as a cast fitting. Since the composition of fittings varies from 85 to 95 per cent copper, there is a saving of about 35 to 45 per cent in copper alone, besides the zinc, tin, and other metals used.

These special fittings have proved to be very satisfactory in service in spite of their light weight and streamlined appearance, since they are as strong as, or even stronger than, the pipe lines to which they are attached.

# CHAPTER XVII

## SHIPWORK

Shipwork may be divided into two groups, repair and new construction. The difference between the two is that in new construction the ship does not yet have a crew, and the machinery and piping are in the process of being installed. Repair work is done on ships that have been in service.

**New Construction.**—A ship may be built either in a dry dock or on a building ways. A ship built in a dry dock is laid down to a true level, whereas the ships constructed on ways are usually built while they are on a sloping fore-and-aft angle. For this reason the ships built on ways need special leveling devices. Usually a wedge-shaped level is made to compensate for the angle at which the ship is tilted on the ways. The pipe systems and ship's structure are leveled to these special levels so that, when the ship is launched, they will be on an even keel in line with the ship structure. In a dry dock the special level is not necessary because the ship being built is level. But once the ship is launched, all leveling must be done by measurements and sight. The level is used only when the ship is in a building dock or on the ways.

Ships under new construction are built entirely from plans; therefore it is necessary for the mechanic to understand blueprints. The measurements given on the plans must be followed to a very close tolerance, because they allow for the installation of machinery and also follow the plan of the ship.

Close coordination with other crafts is also very important, in order to put the work in at the most efficient stage of construction and to facilitate any slight alterations of construction that may vary from the plan.

The piping templates are usually bent from the layout given on detailed blueprints, and they are checked aboard ship before the pipe is bent. If blueprints are not available, the template may be bent to the mechanic's own detailed drawings made from the three views given on the plans. Checking all templates aboard ship before bending the pipe is always a good practice.

**Repair.**—The crew on board ship has charge of operating the machinery, and the workmen repair the equipment as instructed. The instructions for the repairs are usually obtained by the shop foreman from the planning and estimating division and signed by the shop superintendent. These instructions are called "job orders"; they contain explanations of all repairs and alterations that are to take place, and they also contain references to the necessary blueprints.

Before the mechanic starts to work on piping systems, the safe thing to do is to find out from the member of the ship's force who is in charge of that particular system if the system is empty and ready to be dismantled. Every precaution should be taken that no pipe joints are dismantled without proper authorization and that the line is not charged. The crew usually removes the liquids or the pressure from lines, preparing them for dismantling. When the lines are removed, steel blanks should be placed on all pipe and valve openings to prevent damage or flooding of the ship through accidental valve opening and to prevent foreign objects from falling into the machinery or valves.

Before lines on a ship are dismantled, they should have metal tags wired on them with strong wire. The tag should have sufficient information on it to enable another mechanic to install it, for example, job order, location of pipe aboard ship, system, and ship's name. Sometimes pipes are left for weeks before they can be reinstalled, and, if the pipes were not properly marked, there would be much confusion and loss of time when they were put back.

Tags of sheet copper or sheet steel about 2 by 3 in. should be made for each pipe. The lettering is punched into the tag with a metal stencil punch. This type of tag can stand heat, acid, or any treatment that the coppersmith may give it while the pipe is being repaired. The flanges on adjoining pipes should be marked by center-punch or chisel marks to facilitate matching for reassembling pipes.

Every effort should be made to cooperate with the crew; when you are dismantling lines, see that the liquids remaining in low spots of pipes do not spill or splash indiscriminately. Always remember that the ship is the sailor's home; he lives there, and all unnecessary dirt or litter must be cleaned up by him.

**General Information.**—The officer of the deck is responsible for all activities aboard ship.   If you are in doubt about any condition or situation, or if information is desired concerning locked storerooms, compartments, tanks, pipe lines, etc., the officer of the deck will tell you where to find the men responsible for them.   He stands his watch on the quarter-deck in view of the ship's ladder or gangway and checks the arrival and departure of all traffic to and from the ship.

**Fire Watch.**—Safety precautions must be observed when the workmen are using open flame of any sort aboard ship.   The officer of the deck must be notified before the torches are lit, so that a fire watch may be assigned by him to stand by with fire-fighting equipment.   No torches should be used unless the fire watch is present and ready.   The vicinity where the open flame is to be used should be cleared of all inflammables.   Never take a chance where the safety of the ship is concerned.

**Sea Valves.**—The sea valves are connected either to the side or the bottom of a ship.   Great care should be exercised when removing piping connected to the sea valve.   The valve should be closed tightly and then secured with a chain and either locked or wired shut.   It should always be blanked off when pipe is not actually being fitted to it.

**Line Markings.**—Except in isolated cases, all pipe lines are painted with identification bands encircling the pipe in order that the lines may be identified at a glance.   In some locations aboard ship, the different systems converge at one point, and quick identification is possible only when the lines are marked (see Fig. 60).

**Making up and Installing Lines.**—When you are installing aboard ship a line that consists of several sections, the sections should never be set up and tightened individually.   The complete line with all its sections should first be set into place and the bolts tightened finger tight at each flange.   Then two or three opposite bolts should be pulled up at each pair of flanges, tightly enough to face the flange evenly.   When all flanges are faced evenly, the bolts should be tightened at diametric opposites to ensure an even tension on the flange facing.

| SERVICE | | COLORS |
|---|---|---|
| GAS | Compressed air | One yellow band |
| | Ventilating air | Two yellow bands |
| | Refrigerating gases | Three yellow bands |
| FIRE EXTINGUISHING (Other than water) | All regardless of chemical used | One brown band |
| HYDRAULIC | Power | One blue band |
| | Control | Two blue bands |
| OIL | Fuel | One red band |
| | Diesel | One red band with white "D" |
| | Gasoline | Entire line and fittings painted red |
| | Kerosene | One red band with white "K" |
| | Lubricating | Three red bands |
| STEAM | Supply | One black band |
| | Exhaust | Two black bands |
| WATER | Drainage and drains | One green band |
| | Fire | Two green bands |
| | Flushing, Flooding, Sprinkling, and circulating | Three green bands |
| | Fresh water | Four green bands |
| | Brine | Five green bands |

One stripe, two inches wide, more than one stripe, one inch wide
Each pipe shall have at least one striping designation in each compartment through which it passes
Identification bands shall not be placed on flanges, fittings, or valves
Pipes in cabins, officer's wardroom, and messrooms, and in warrant officers' messrooms shall not be striped
The body of pipes shall be painted the same color as that of the adjacent bulkheads and decks
Galvanized metal pipe lagging shall not be painted nor striped
Vessels carrying both Diesel and Boiler oil shall have a white "D" stenciled on the band on Diesel oil pipes

FIG. 60.—System identifications.

**Measurements Aboard Ship.**—The measurements aboard ship are taken from fixed points, such as center line, base line, bulkheads, overhead, deck, and frames. Some plans use machinery or other equipment as measuring points aboard ship.

**Clearances Allowed for Lagging.**—All steam, exhaust, water, plumbing, and refrigeration lines aboard ship are covered with special covering materials. The steam lines are covered with asbestos covering varying from 1 to 6 in., depending on the amount of heat in the line. Water and plumbing lines are covered with hair-felt covering about 1 in. thick to prevent accumulation of moisture on the outside of the pipe due to condensation. Refrigeration supply lines are covered with cork 2 to 3 in. thick.

**Gaskets.**—Gaskets of different types are necessary when flanged joints are being made on piping and machinery. The gasket is primarily a filler between two imperfect joints. Theoretically, if the flanged joints were perfectly faced and aligned, a gasket would be unnecessary; however, the time required to spot-face a flange to the perfection needed for a leakproof joint makes it preferable to use a gasket.

The type of gasket material used depends on the service of the line and also on what pressure it will be subjected to (see Table XVII). A few types of gasket material used are metal for extreme high pressures, asbestos for low-pressure steam and general use, rubber for cold water, and plant fiber for oil and gasoline. The gasket material is available in sheet form, and the gaskets are cut to the required size and shape.

**Making a Gasket.**—To mark a gasket for cutting, lay a flange on the gasket material and then mark the shape of the gasket through the flange. When all the boltholes and the inside and outside diameters of the flange are marked onto the gasket, remove the flange and punch the holes with a gasket punch. The holes should be about $\frac{1}{16}$ in. larger than the bolts to be used. Then cut the material with snips, scissors, or a knife.

**Grommets.**—The grommet is a soft washer. Grommets are made from cotton wicking and are used mostly on bulkhead flanges and on flanges connected to bulkhead flanges to make the boltholes watertight. The grommets are made by wrapping the cotton wicking around a finger or an object of the required size, then making a series of half hitches around the wrapped circle

TABLE XVII.—GASKET RECOMMENDATIONS—GENERAL SPECIFICATIONS
FOR MACHINERY, NAVY DEPARTMENT

| Service | Pressure, lb. | Temp., °F. | Gasket materials |
|---|---|---|---|
| Steam saturated, low pressure... | ........ | 265 | Compressed-asbestos sheet<br>Asbestos metallic-cloth sheet<br>Spiral-wound metal asbestos gasket |
| Steam saturated, medium pressure...................... | To 300 | To 425 | Compressed-asbestos sheet<br>Spiral-wound metal asbestos gasket<br>Serrated or plain metal gaskets<br>Asbestos metallic-cloth sheet |
| Steam, superheated and saturated high pressure........... | 300 to 600 | 720 | Spiral-wound metal gasket<br>Serrated or plain metal gaskets<br>Metal-to-metal joints |
| Water, cold, fresh, salt, and brine, low and high pressure........ | To 250 | 120 | Compressed-asbestos sheet<br>Asbestos metallic-cloth sheet<br>Rubber-sheet, cloth insertion<br>Rubber-sheet, wire insertion<br>Spiral-wound metal asbestos gasket |
| Water, hot, fresh, salt, and brine, low and high pressure........ | To 600 | 250 | Compressed-asbestos sheet<br>Asbestos metallic-cloth sheet<br>Rubber-sheet wire insertion<br>Spiral-wound metal asbestos gasket<br>Serrated or plain metal gaskets |
| Air, low pressure............... | To 200 | ..... | Compressed-asbestos sheet<br>Rubber-sheet cloth insertion |
| Gas, sulphur dioxide........... | To 100 | ..... | Rubber-sheet wire insertion |
| Gas, ethyl chloride............. | To 50 | ..... | Spiral-wound metal asbestos gasket |
| Gas, ammonia................. | To 100 | ..... | Serrated or plain metal gasket |
| Gas, dichloro, difluoro, methane, freon...................... | To 175 | ..... | Compressed-asbestos sheet<br>Serrated or plain metal gaskets |
| Air, high pressure.............. | ........ | ..... | Spiral-wound metal asbestos gasket<br>Metal-to-metal joints |
| Gas, carbon dioxide............ | To 1,500 | ..... | Hard-fiber sheet<br>Spiral-wound metal asbestos gasket<br>Serrated or plain metal gaskets |
| Oil, fuel, suction............... | To 100 | 130 | Plant-fiber sheet<br>Spiral-wound metal asbestos gasket<br>Serrated or plain metal gasket |
| Gasoline...................... | To 50 | ..... | Plant-fiber sheet<br>Spiral-wound metal asbestos gasket<br>Serrated or plain metal gaskets |
| Oil, lubricating................ | To 150 | 180 | Plant-fiber sheet<br>Spiral-wound metal asbestos gasket<br>Serrated or plain metal gaskets |
| Gases, of combustion........... | To 500 | 720 | Compressed-asbestos gasket<br>Asbestos metallic cloth sheet<br>Spiral-wound metal asbestos gasket<br>Serrated or plain metal gaskets |
| Oil, fuel, discharge............. | To 400 | 210 | Compressed-asbestos sheet<br>Spiral-wound metal asbestos gasket<br>Serrated or plain metal gaskets<br>Metal-to-metal joints |

until the grommet is firm. Before installation the grommet should be saturated in red lead.

**Working in Tanks.**—**Never work in a tank alone, especially when using an oxyacetylene torch.** A fire watch must always be present with the necessary fire-fighting equipment. All inflammables should be removed from the area of flame. The torch and hose must be tested at the bottles for leaks before being taken into the tank. The hose must be strung carefully so that it will not be cut accidentally. A helper should be stationed near the oxygen and acetylene flasks to shut them off quickly in case of an accident.

If work is to be done inside tanks that have been freshly painted or in oil tanks that have been cleaned and steamed, a chemist's O.K. must first be obtained before they are entered. The chemist's O.K. should be placed on a board and hung at each tank opening together with a record of inspection, including the time of inspection. The record should state how often the tank should be tested.

**Cutting Orders.**—Whenever it is necessary to cut holes through bulkheads, frames, or decks, the mechanic must obtain and fill out a cutting-order form. This form has to be filled out to show where the holes are; what size they are; how many there are; forward or aft of what frames; whether they are on the port or starboard side; how far they are from the center line of the ship; which deck or platform they are on; whether the holes are to be drilled, burned, or cut with a chipping gun, etc.

After the form has been signed by the coppersmith leadingman and the ship superintendent, it is given to the driller leadingman or welder leadingman or chipper-and-calker leadingman, depending on which trade is to make the holes. This cutting order, properly signed, authorizes the mechanic to go ahead with the job. Never make holes in any part of the ship's structure without proper authority.

**Testing Aboard Ship.**—The first step in testing systems aboard ship is to read test specifications and then to study the system thoroughly. Isolate all machinery, pumps, condensers, tanks, etc., unless otherwise noted in the test specifications. Make sure that the valves that must be closed are wired shut and then tagged so that accidental opening is impossible. Check to make sure that all bosses have plugs in them. Check on all bolted and screwed joints and unions. Tighten packing nuts on valves. Insert the pressure and then check for leaks.

**Drop Test.**—A drop test is used after all visible leaks have been corrected. A gauge or several gauges are set up at different parts of the system that is being tested, water or air is injected into the lines, and a reading is taken after the required pressure is in the line. The filling connections are removed after the system is full. If the gauge shows a drop after the filling connections have been removed, there is leakage somewhere, and the leaks must be located either by soap-and-water applications to air pipes or by a visual test of water pipes.

**Testing a High-pressure Air System.**—High-pressure air lines aboard ship are first tested with water at 5,000 lb. per sq. in. The system is blanked off into sections that are tested individually. If these tests are successful, the water is removed, and the sections are tested with air. Soap is used on all joints and connections in order to find leaks. Whenever a leak is found, the spot is tagged. After the section has been checked and the leaks tagged, the air is bled from the system; then the leaks are taken care of. **Never tighten leaks on high-pressure air lines when lines are charged with air.**

After the leaks have been tightened, the line is again charged with air to the operating pressure, which varies from 2,000 to 3,000 lb. per sq. in. on different ships. The system is then ready for the drop test. The drop test is usually an 8-hr. test with a specified drop allowance. If the system drops more than the allowable drop, hunt for the leaks, using soap water to find them.

**Always test sections of a system individually to begin with; then, after the various sections have been tested individually, the complete system is cut in and tested.**

**Testing a Low-Pressure Air System.**—The low-pressure air system aboard ship is usually tested only with air at its operating pressure of about 100 lb. per sq. in. The pressure is injected slowly at first until the larger leaks have been tightened. After the large leaks have been corrected, the drop test is begun and the smaller leaks are corrected until the system is tight.

**Freon Testing.**—Testing Freon refrigerator systems is done by first injecting 25 lb. of Freon into the system and then looking for the leaks by means of soap and water or halide lamps. (The halide lamp is a small torch that is fueled either with alcohol or with acetylene. It has a hose attachment that draws in air to supply the torch, and, when this hose is put near a leaking joint, it draws in the acetylene gas, changing the ordinary white flame to a blue-green flame.) When no leaks are found with 25 lb. of Freon, either nitrogen or $CO_2$ is added until the pressure reaches 225 lb. per sq. in. A halide lamp and soap and water are again used. When all visible leaks have been taken care of and the gauge shows no drop during the required test period, the drop test is made.

**Systems Aboard Ship.**—When a coppersmith is installing pipe on board ship, he finds it valuable to have at least a brief working knowledge of the various piping systems. It should be the aim of every coppersmith to learn as much as he can about the operation of the system he is installing. The information given here is merely a starting point for the new man. The workman may obtain further information concerning the operation and theory of the various systems by studying the blueprints. A study of the blueprints and material list will generally reveal the operation of a system.

**Lubricating-oil Lines.**—Lubricating-oil lines aboard modern vessels are usually made of copper material because copper is easily worked and is therefore suitable for these lines, which require many branches and sharp bends. Since the weight factor is very important in shipbuilding, copper has an advantage over other metals because it is lighter.

The lubricating oil is carried to the various machines and engines and must therefore be free of scale and dirt. Great care must be exercised to prevent foreign substances from entering the lines when they are being installed, and the nonrusting, non-scaling properties of copper make it valuable for this purpose. After fabrication, but before installation aboard ship, the lines should be cleaned and treated so that all traces of acid, scale, and dirt are removed.

Lubricating-oil lines are usually tested in the shop by means of water and air and then given an air test on board ship when the line is installed.

**Gasoline Lines.**—Gasoline lines carry the gasoline from the storage tanks to the service outlets. They are made of either steel, copper, or copper-nickel alloy.

Gasoline is not always pumped mechanically; sometimes it is forced through the system by gravity. Salt water is pumped into the gasoline-storage tank, forcing the gasoline to the service outlets. Because gasoline is lighter than water, it floats on the surface of the water. When the salt water is pumped into the tank, the gasoline is forced upward and out into the gasoline outlets. The line of demarcation where the water and gasoline meet is called the "cleavage line." A float on this cleavage line raises and lowers the gauges, showing the level of the gasoline. When the float rises to the top, the tank is empty; when it lowers, the tank is full of gasoline.

Gasoline lines are drop tested with air. Sometimes they are tested for seepage by being filled with kerosene.

**Diesel Oil.**—Diesel-oil lines are usually made of steel. They carry diesel oil from the storage tanks to the diesel engines. Diesel oil is very difficult to hold because it is very penetrating. The pipe joints must be carefully fitted, and the facings of flanges and unions must be free from scale and grit.

All diesel-oil installations are tested with air before and after installation.

**Fuel-oil Lines.**—Fuel-oil lines are usually made of steel. They supply the boilers with fuel. Since the fuel-oil lines are similar to the diesel-oil lines, the same precautions against leaks are necessary.

All oil and gasoline lines are tested similarly.

**Main Steam Lines.**—Steel lines with Van Stone flanges are used in modern ships for high-pressure steam lines. The main steam line supplies steam from the boilers to the steam engines and turbines. These lines must have a maximum flexibility to allow for the expansion and contraction caused by the heating and cooling of the steam. Wherever possible, expansion bends should be incorporated in the lines.

Testing usually consists of a shop hydrostatic test and an installation hydrostatic drop test aboard ship.

**Auxiliary Steam Lines.**—Most of these systems are constructed of steel. Auxiliary steam serves all auxiliary machinery, such as pumps, blowers, galley, steam radiators, whistles. Regulating valves adjust the pressure to whatever amount is needed to operate the individual machinery or the systems.

All steam lines must be free of dips or pockets where water might accumulate.

Testing usually consists of shop and ship hydrostatic tests.

**Steam Heat.**—Copper pipes are used to carry steam to the various heating units throughout the ship. Steam heat is usually supplied to the ship by means of an individual system connected to auxiliary steam or to a steam-heat boiler unit. Pockets or dips are avoided because they collect moisture, which must be bled off by individual steam-drain connections. Special insulated bulkhead fittings are used to insulate the hot pipe from the bulkheads. (See Bulkhead Flange Detail, Fig. 9.)

Testing consists of installation tests and hydrostatic and air drop tests.

**Steam Drains.**—High-pressure steam-drain lines are usually made of steel, low-pressure drains of copper. Steam drains remove the condensate from low spots in steam lines or from the outlets of steam-heating units.

Steam lines have a certain amount of condensate, or moisture, especially if there are pockets in the line. This condensate is usually eliminated by means of steam drains. Steam heat drains have a steam trap valve that eliminates condensate automatically whenever it accumulates.

Installation tests are usually hydrostatic.

**Auxiliary Exhaust.**—The exhaust lines, usually made of copper, draw the steam exhaust from the auxiliary machinery into the condensers. It is necessary to allow for expansion and contraction by installing sufficient expansion bends or expansion joints. Bulkhead flanges should be insulated from the bulkhead.

Testing consists of a shop hydrostatic test and an operation test.

**Refrigeration Systems.**—Copper piping is used throughout on modern refrigeration systems. Copper tees and special nonporous valves are also used to ensure against leakage of refrigerant gas.

These lines carry refrigerant from the compressors to the refrigerating boxes. Special care must be taken so that no moisture or dirt particles remain in the system after installation. (See Freon Testing, page 175, for test instructions.)

**High-pressure Air Lines.**—A high-pressure air system is constructed of copper material about $5/8$ in. O.D. of especially heavy wall thickness. Besides supplying air to the guns for counterrecoil, torpedo tubes, and airplane catapults, it is also tied in with low-pressure air systems, the gas-ejection system, and diesel-starting air systems, which it can supply through reducing valves in case these separate systems fail. The high-pressure air system operates between 2,000 and 3,000 lb. per sq. in.

**Gas-ejection System.**—Copper is often used in the construction of these systems. The gas-ejection system is used to blow powder gases away from the gun barrels after each shot, in order to prevent accidental ignition when powder bags are inserted into the breech.

These lines should be tested similarly to low-pressure air lines.

**Low-pressure Air Lines.**—Copper piping is used throughout these lines. Low-pressure air has many uses. It is the source of power for pneumatic tools and for general cleaning service throughout the ship. The operating pressure of low-pressure air is about 100 lb. per sq. in.

**Fire Main.**—Because of the strongly corrosive action of salt water, either lead-lined steel pipe, copper pipe coated inside with wiping metal, or copper-nickel alloy should be used. The primary purpose of the fire main aboard ship is to fight fire. The main problem presented by this line is the corrosion caused by the salt water that it carries.

Testing consists of shop hydrostatic and ship installation air and water tests.

**Flushing Lines.**—Copper-nickel alloy, lead-lined steel, and tinned and wiped copper piping are used for this type of line. Salt-water flushing lines serve all heads and toilets throughout the ship, the salt water being usually supplied from the fire main or flushing pumps.

Just as in the fire main lines, the greatest problem is the corrosion caused by the salt water.

Tests consist of shop hydrostatic and an operating test after installation.

**Evaporator System.**—The evaporator plant aboard ship separates the salt from sea water, making the water fit for use as drinking water, for the boilers, and for operating ship's machinery. Salt water cannot be used in the steam boilers because of the salt deposits in the machinery and because of the corrosive action of salt water on metals.

The evaporator is merely a distilling unit that is built especially for salt-water distilling. Steam from exhaust or auxiliary systems supplies the heat for the distilling process.  The steam goes through a series of small tubes in the evaporator shell that are covered with salt water.  The salt water is heated to the boiling point by the hot tubes, the first effect; and then the vaporized salt water is condensed and distilled again, the second effect. Some large systems have a third effect.  The salt remains at the bottom of the tube nest and is pumped back into the sea through lines called "brine lines."

The evaporator system is essential because a ship with an evaporator can stay at sea indefinitely, or at least until its fuel runs out, but a ship without an evaporator must carry all its water in storage tanks, and its stay at sea is limited by the amount of water carried.

Copper and copper-nickel alloy tubing are used almost entirely throughout the evaporator system.

**Cooling-water Lines.**—The fluid used to cool bearings, condensers, and oil coolers is cold water, either fresh or salt.  These lines, for salt water, are usually of tinned and wiped copper or of copper nickel.

The water does not go directly into the oil; it is piped through coils or tubes that are set into the oil reservoir.  The cold water passing through the tubes cools the oil.  This principle, in general, is called a "heat exchange."

**Brine Lines.**—Tinned- and wiped-copper or copper-nickel lines are used to construct the brine lines that carry the brine overboard from the evaporator plants.  The corrosion caused by the salt-water action and the heavy salt deposits that clog the pipes are the main problems.

Testing consists of shop hydraulic and ship operating tests.

**Fresh-water Lines.**—The material for fresh-water lines may be copper, brass, or steel, as there is no excessive corrosion present. Fresh water is manufactured from sea water.  It is used in the steam boilers of the ship as well as for drinking and bathing purposes by the crew.  There is little corrosion present in fresh-water lines.

Testing usually consists of a shop hydrostatic test followed by a ship hydrostatic test after installation.

**Hydraulic Piping.**—Both copper and steel are used in the construction of these lines.  Hydraulic lines connect the machinery that is operated hydraulically.  Since this machinery is very delicate and must be kept very clean, the openings to the machinery should be kept closed at all times, unless piping is actually being fitted to it. A special cleaning procedure must be followed when hydraulic piping is prepared for installation (see Hydraulic Pipe-cleaning Process, page 17).

Testing consists of shop hydrostatic tests and an operation test after installation.

**Safety.**—Always use stagings, not boxes or portable makeshifts. Riggers will build staging aboard ship when necessary; do not build temporary staging yourself. Do not play or jump on staging. Keep your place of work clean; do not let tools lie around, especially when working aboard ship or on staging.

Do not play with compressed air. It is dangerous. Do not use compressed air to clean your clothing or place of work, because the terrific blast may blow small particles of metal, etc., with enough force to put out an eye or to imbed the particles in the flesh of a fellow workman several feet away.

Always insist on ventilation suckers or blowers when working with or near welders, especially when they are welding galvanized iron. Be careful when working near welders that you do not look into the welding arc. It may cause serious injury to the eyes. Wear dark goggles when working near welders. Goggles to be worn while you are either near welders or performing acetylene welding or burning should be shade 3 or 4; for arc welding use 8, 10, or 12.

Do not use an open flame or weld on oil tanks or near oil tanks.

Always be on the alert for crane loads overhead. Keep out from underneath. Keep manhole safety covers on tanks to prevent accidents. When lights go out, do not move about; stay where you are. Report unsafe conditions to your supervisor.

If you are not familiar with certain equipment, tools, or machinery, get help from the proper authorities before using them. Use safe tools. Do not use cracked or broken equipment. Always grind mushrooms from striking tools such as chisels, wedges, center punches, and hammers, or return the mushroomed tools to the toolroom for repair.

Always use the toilet facilities provided. *Never* urinate in ship bilges or compartments. Spitting or committing any other nuisance is strictly forbidden.

# CHAPTER XVIII

## COMPARTMENTATION

In addition to working in the shop the coppersmith, as has been noted, must also work aboard ship; for this reason he should know something about finding his way around a ship. He should familiarize himself with ship's terms, label abbreviations, decks, deck numbering, compartments, compartment numbering, measuring points, and all general information about the structure of a ship.

Figure 61 shows a simple sketch of a typical arrangement of large ships. Smaller ships, of course, do not have so many decks; therefore it is simpler to find your way around. It is easy to get directions confused when you are busy working below deck. In such a case, if the frame-numbering system is known, it is easy to determine your immediate location.

Some of the larger ships are 700 or 800 ft. long, over 100 ft. wide, and have a height of 8 or 9 stories or more; therefore they can readily be compared to a large, complicated hotel building that has hundreds of rooms and numerous passageways.

Many piping systems are run through only one or two compartments, but some systems are run through the complete length of the ship, including most of the decks. The following brief outline will aid one to secure a mental picture of most ships.[1]

**Ship's Decks.**—The *main deck* is the highest of the decks extending completely from the bow to the stern.

The *forecastle deck* is the partial deck above the main deck at the bow.

The *poop deck* is the partial deck above the main deck at the stern.

The *superstructure deck*, usually located amidships, is the partial deck above the forecastle; it does not extend to the extreme sides of the ship.

---

[1] The author wishes to acknowledge his indebtedness for much of the material in this chapter to the Navy Department's pamphlet *Nomenclature of Naval Vessels* published June, 1941, in Washington, D.C.

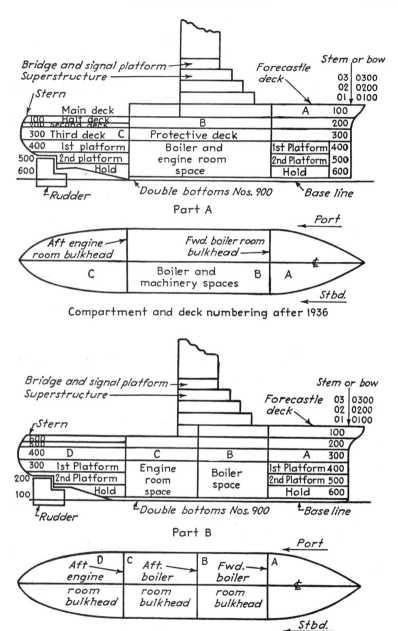

Part A

Compartment and deck numbering after 1936

Part B

Compartment and deck numbering before 1936

FIG. 61.—Ship compartmentation.

The *second deck* is the first full deck below the main deck.

On some ships there are two or more complete decks below the main deck; they are named the *second, third, fourth decks,* etc.

*Half decks* are partial decks between the lowest complete deck and the main deck.

The *platform deck* is the partial deck below the lowest complete deck.

Where there are two or more partial decks below the lowest complete deck, they are named the *first platform, second platform,* etc.

Decks that for protective purposes are fitted with plating of extra heaviness and strength are named *protective* and *splinter decks* in addition to their regular names.

The *protective deck* is named such when it is the only deck of extra-heavy thickness aboard the ship.

The *splinter deck* is named such when there are two protective decks; it is the heavier deck of the two.

**Ship Divisions. Ships Built before 1936** (see Fig. 61*B*).—Division *A* is the space between the bow and the forward bulkhead of the forward boiler room.

Division *B* is the space between the forward and after bulkheads of the forward boiler room.

Division *C* is the space between the after and forward bulkheads of the after engine spaces.

Division *D* is the space aft of the after bulkhead of the after engine room.

**Ship Divisions. Ships Built after 1936** (see Fig. 61).—Division *A* is the space between the stem and the forward bulkhead of the forward machinery compartment.

Division *B* is the space between the forward bulkhead of the forward machinery compartment and the after bulkhead of the after machinery compartment.

Division *C* is the space aft of the after bulkhead of the after machinery compartment.

The *machinery compartments* are the boiler rooms, engine rooms, main motor rooms, and compartments containing auxiliaries of the main propelling machinery.

**Key to Numbering.**—Numbering of each division begins at the forward end of that division.

COMPARTMENTATION185

Compartments on the starboard side of the ship have odd numbers; those on the port side have even numbers.

Compartments and spaces that are watertight, oiltight, airtight, or fumetight are numbered.

On the main deck oiltight and watertight compartments are numbered from 101 to 199; those on each deck or platform below the main deck are numbered consecutively in the next higher hundred series. Thus the second deck is numbered from 201 to 299, the third deck from 301 to 399, etc.

The watertight compartments on the deck or platform immediately above the main deck are numbered 0101 to 0199, and those on the next higher decks are numbered in the next higher hundred series also prefixed with a zero.

For instance: a ship with a superstructure, forecastle, main, second, and third decks, and first and second platform decks would be numbered as follows:

| | |
|---|---|
| Superstructure deck.......................... | 0201–0299 |
| Forecastle deck............................. | 0101–0199 |
| Main deck................................. | 101– 199 |
| Second deck............................... | 201– 299 |
| Third deck................................ | 301– 399 |
| First platform............................. | 401– 499 |
| Second platform........................... | 501– 599 |
| Hold...................................... | 601– 699 |
| Double bottoms............................ | 901– 999 |

The numbering of decks in the foregoing is true of ships built after 1936. For those built before 1936, the decks are numbered from the hold up as follows:

| | |
|---|---|
| Hold...................................... | 101– 199 |
| Second platform........................... | 201– 299 |
| First platform............................. | 301– 399 |
| Third deck................................ | 401– 499 |
| Second deck............................... | 501– 599 |
| Main deck................................. | 601– 699 |
| Forecastle deck............................ | 0101–0199 |
| Superstructure deck........................ | 0201–0299 |

On modern destroyers the compartment numbers are thus:

| | |
|---|---|
| Main deck................................. | 101–199 |
| First platform............................. | 201–299 |
| Second platform........................... | 301–399 |
| Hold...................................... | 401–499 |

The rest of the numbering is similar to that in both the other types of ship.

**Label Plates.**—Brass plates, inscribed with the number and name of the enclosure, are fitted to the ship's doors, hatches, and tank openings.   The number of the compartment is prefixed by a letter which indicates the general division of the ship; the number and letter are separated by a hyphen.

The compartment number is followed by a designating letter:

*A* for storerooms, refrigerator compartments, tool and supply rooms, and compartments to be used as storerooms.

*B* for battery compartments, namely, torpedo rooms, compartments within turrets, and handling rooms.

*C* for ship-control and fire-control compartments, namely, central, coding room, interior communication, main communication station, plotting room, radio rooms, switchboard rooms, and torpedo racking room.

*E* for machinery compartments, namely, blower room, boiler room, evaporator room, workshop, main engine room, main motor room, laundry, pump room, shaft alley, steering-gear room, etc.

*F* for fuel compartments, namely, diesel oil compartments, relay-tank room, etc.

*LUB* for lubricating-oil storage tanks.

*GAS* for gasoline compartments.

*L* for living compartments, namely, crew's spaces, officers' quarters, etc.

*M* for ammunition spaces, namely, bomb magazines, handling rooms, etc.

*T* for trunks and passages having numbers.

*V* for void compartments, namely, cofferdam compartments, void double-bottom compartments, etc.

*W* for water compartments, namely, drainage tanks, fresh-water compartments, peak tanks, reserve-feed compartments, etc.

*Example*: C-205-L means a living compartment on the starboard side of the second deck in *C* division (see Fig. 61).

**Inscription Plates.**—Inscription plates give the number, compartment description, and compartment number of the door, hatch, or manhole to which they are attached; they are combined with capacity plates whenever possible.

**Frame Numbers and Bulkheads.**—At least every fifth frame is numbered in the principal living compartments and wherever necessary elsewhere. Frame numbers are combined with door numbers wherever possible.

Each transverse bulkhead has at least one number plate in each compartment—also combined with door plates wherever possible.

**Other Label Plates.**—Plates are installed on bulkheads in nearly every compartment and show the center lines and heights from the base line for obtaining accurate measurements from base lines and center lines. These plates are either circular or cross shaped and made of brass.

Capacity plates are combined with door, hatch, or compartment numbers wherever possible.

ABBREVIATIONS FOUND ON LABEL PLATES

| | |
|---|---|
| Amm | Ammunition |
| A. T. | Airtight |
| Aux. | Auxiliary |
| B. H. | Bulkhead |
| C & R | Construction and Repair |
| Circ | Circulating |
| Comp't | Compartment |
| C. P. O. | Chief Petty Officer |
| Cu. Ft. | Cubic feet |
| Dis. | Discharge |
| E. | Engineering |
| Elec | Electric |
| Equip | Equipment |
| Evap | Evaporator |
| For'd | Forward |
| F. O. | Fuel oil |
| F. T. | Fumetight |
| Ft. | Feet or foot |
| F. W. | Fresh water |
| Gals | Gallons |
| In | Inches |
| J. O. | Junior Officers |
| Lub | Lubricating oil |
| Mag | Magazines |
| M. H. | Manhole |
| Med | Medical |
| M. T. | Flametight |
| Nav | Navigation |
| N. T. | Nontight |
| Offs | Officers |

Ord...................... Ordnance
O. T...................... Oiltight
Ready S. Mag............. Ready service magazine
Salut. Pwdr.............. Saluting powder
S. D...................... Supply department
Sergt.................... Sergeant
Stbd..................... Starboard
Suc...................... Suction
T........................ Tons
Torp..................... Torpedo
Trans.................... Transverse
Vent..................... Ventilation
V. T..................... Voice tube
W........................ Weathertight
W. C..................... Water closet
W. L..................... Water line
W. O..................... Warrant Officer
W. R..................... Ward room
W. T..................... Watertight

## SHIP'S TERMS

**Aft** (after)—toward the stern.

**Air port or porthole**—a small round window in the side of the ship, fitted with a thick plate of glass.

**Amidships**—on the center line of the ship, at the point halfway between the bow and the stern.

**Athwart**—pertaining to lines running from port to starboard side, such as, athwart ship's beams and bulkheads, differentiating from longitudinal beams.

**Base line**—a reference line running fore and aft, for vertical measurements laid down on the keel of the ship.

**Beams**—athwart ship frames.

**Bilge**—the inside bottom of the ship generally underneath the engine-room floor plates.

**Bow**—the forward end of the ship.

**Bulkhead**—a division of the ship, comparable to a wall in a hotel.

**Center line**—the horizontal line running fore and aft which divides the port from the starboard side.

**Deck**—the floor of the ship.

**Fantail**—the overhang of the ship at the stern.

**Frames**—athwart ship beams. (See Athwart.)

**Hull**—the main body of the ship, excluding the superstructure.

**Inboard**—toward the center line from either the port or the starboard side.

**Keel**—the lowest longitudinal frame running completely fore and aft at the center line of the ship. The frames are attached to it.

**Magazine**—ammunition stowage.

**Manhole**—a hole designed to allow entrance into tanks, condenser heads, compartments, etc., for inspection and repairs.

**Midships**—see Amidships.

**Port side**—the left-hand side of the ship when looking toward the bow.

**Scuppers**—openings in the sides of the ship which permit the water to run off the decks.

**Stanchion**—an iron post standing vertically and supporting the weight on the decks.

**Starboard**—the right-hand side of the ship when looking forward.

**Superstructure**—any structure built above the main body or hull.

**Transverse**—abeam, athwart, or crosswise of the ship.

**Water lines**—the distance from the base line upward, marked inside of the ship on each deck at the center line on the bulkheads to aid in finding measurements.

# INDEX